HORROR MOVIES BINGE VOL. 2

WES LAURIE

Books by Wes Laurie

Movies Binge
Crap Poetry
Action Movies Binge
Horror Movies Binge
Hot Smut
Hollywood Blood Fetish
Florida Man Beyond
Soaked in Madness
Melody
Bad Man
Point X
Burn City
The Taboo - Stories
I Burn and other Stories
Psexycho
America Goes to the Movies: the 1980s
America Goes to the Movies: the 1990s
The Monster Game
The House Under Hell
Beerasaurus Sex

HORROR MOVIES BINGE VOL. 2

Wes Laurie

The 50 movies in this binge:

1. M3GAN
2. EVIL DEAD RISE
3. PEARL
4. X
5. MEN
6. THE MUMMY
7. LIFEFORCE
8. INFINITY POOL
9. DEMON KNIGHT
10. FIVE NIGHTS AT FREDDY'S
11. ZOMBIELAND
12. SLEEPY HOLLOW
13. FRANKENSTEIN
14. BARBARIAN
15. PSYCHO
16. IT
17. BONES AND ALL
18. THE WOLFMAN
19. MALEVOLENT
20. IT'S ALIVE
21. THE WRAITH
22. AFTER MIDNIGHT
23. WILLY'S WONDERLAND
24. SCREAM
25. SCREAM 2
26. SCREAM 3
27. SCREAM 4
28. SCREAM (5)
29. SCREAM 6
30. THE LAST VOYAGE OF THE DEMETER
31. VIDEODROME
32. NIGHTMARE CINEMA
33. ALIEN

34. DISTURBIA
35. PET SEMATARY: BLOODLINES
36. THE WOMAN IN BLACK
37. EVENT HORIZON
38. AMERICAN PSYCHO
39. THE EXORCIST: BELIEVER
40. SNOWBEAST
41. LISA FRANKENSTEIN
42. TERRIFIER 2
43. THE MIST
44. BURNT OFFERINGS
45. THE HUNGER
46. NIGHT OF THE LIVING DEAD
47. MANIAC COP
48. NIGHT SWIM
49. AMERICAN PSYCHO 2
50. BLADE

Copyright 2024 by Wes Laurie
ISBN: 9798322704393
Imprint: Independently published
ArsonCuff Press First Edition
Cover Illustration by Wes Laurie

1. M3GAN - 2022

M3gan is a movie based off a material that Akela Cooper and James Wan share the writing credit for; Cooper for screenplay and Wan sharing a Story By credit. Before watching *M3gan* I did not know the production teams involved but afterward when research revealed James Wan's involvement I was not surprised—the vibe fit I think. Wan is known for several series within the horror genre with directing credits that include *Saw*, *Insidious*, and *The Conjuring*. Outside of horror he has helmed big studio superheroes in *Aquaman* and car racing criminals turned heroes in *Furious 7*. James Wan's production company was also behind the horror genre movies *The Nun* and *Annabelle*, amongst others.

Akela Cooper seems to have gotten her start in television writing for shows such as *Tron: Uprising*, *The 100*, and *American Horror Story*. *Hell Fest* is listed as her feature film horror debut. She also wrote on the James Wan directed movie *Malignant*. Akela Cooper was born in the state of Missouri and that fact catches my eye because I too was born in Missouri and it is always interesting to see someone from The Show Me state making a path through Hollywood.

Gerard Johnstone directed *M3gan* with his previous feature being *Housebound* from 2014, which he also wrote.

M3gan features a robotic toy running amok with moral interpretations driven by the artificial intelligence programmed into her by her creator Gemma. Gemma works for a toy company and Megan is meant to be the high-end future of their industry. Testing of the toy comes in the form of Gemma's niece, Cady, who comes to live with her due to her parents dying in a car accident. Cady and Megan become fast friends and Megan takes on the role of protector, a role that evolves as she learns more about how humans treat one another, into a murderous new type of parent.

 Overall, this movie has a story that plays out "as expected" with the build toward horror deaths being somewhat slow. However, Megan the doll is so quirky that it doesn't matter if one can guess most moments to come, weirdness is a draw and entertaining. The movie has serious drama at the core regarding tragedy but the comedy elements are played with flourishes of campiness that somehow felt more natural to the proceedings than not without veering overboard into full-fledged cornball.

 The version of *M3gan* that I watched was the unrated version. I cannot imagine how tame and dull the PG-13 version might be that played at theaters. The marketing team did a decent job when it was released. I think there are enough weird doll moments to have given enough audience members the feeling of "getting their money's worth." I know I was curious about how crazy the film might get based off the trailer showing a silly dance move that Megan performs while stalking a victim down a hall. I grew up watching Chucky kill folks in the *Child's Play* films and I have to point out that if anyone wants to pit the two killer toys against each other I am going to have to side with Team Chucky.

 My favorite moment in the movie is an exchange of

dialog between Gemma and Megan. Gemma says something along the lines of "because you've killed people," to the doll. Megan's reply started with the words "Big whoop." "Big whoop," cracked me up.

Megan kills a woman with a power sprayer. In the version I saw, the pressure from the water tears the woman's cheek open. I guess that moment did not make it into the PG-13 cut. If you are not familiar with power sprayers and wonder if they can do such damage I can attest to the fact that they indeed can. I used to work in a room coating silk screens with emulsion and used a power sprayer to remove old emulsion from screens so that they could be reused. One time I briefly hit my hand with water from the sprayer and indeed lost a tiny chunk of skin.

The acting by the leads in the film is solid with Alison Williams as Gemma and Violet McGraw as Cody. Megan is a character brought to life by the special effects team; however, Jenna Davis did the voice and some of the movements were performed by child actor Amie Donald.

Millen Baird is an actor who plays a police detective for a scene in the movie. It is not a key sort of role but it stood out to me. I found his character amusing, the way they styled his hair helping sell that—little details can leave big impressions. Ha ha.

There were a few sound effects choices that did not blend as well as some other elements for me regarding creative choice. In one scene Megan gets down on all fours to chase after a kid and the galloping sound effects were nonsensical I felt. Later when Megan is held up by some cables in a lab a guy pulls some cords out of her and the air pressure sound effects were also a tad overboard. I am nitpicking. The movie is overall a safe and solid construction with a fun end battle that I guess was going to occur fairly similar to how it indeed did and then a "twist" end that was expected regarding setting up sequels and making a statement on the horrors of modern "smart" technology.

2. EVIL DEAD RISE – 2023

Evil Dead Rise is the fifth film in the *Evil Dead* franchise and was written and directed by Lee Cronin. Before watching this movie, I had never heard of the director before. I have read that this Ireland-born fellow was chosen by Sam Rami after working with him on a series called *50 States of Fright*.

I did not recognize any of the actors featured in this film either, with the leading adult women being Lily Sullivan and Alyssa Sutherland who both hail from Australia. The film itself was shot in New Zealand where producer and director Sam Raimi has been known to stage entertainment industry work which, I am guessing, involves the comfort in connections made when producing long running shows such as *Hercules: The Legendary Journeys* and *Xena: Warrior Princess* that were filmed there.

The entire cast of *Evil Dead Rise* were solid in their performances. I think that Alyssa Sutherland as the possessed Ellie stands out. She is equal parts horrifying, amusing, and sexy as someone possessed by an evil entity. Maybe my opinion on her "sexy" status with her cool tattoos and long legs is going to be shared mostly by others when considering her in pre-possession, but I think that her eyes and wicked smile remained attractive even as her complexion took on sick shades of decomposition.

The story is basic and features some kids who discover the Nature Demonto AKA Necronomicon, The

Book of the Dead in all of its flesh bound and blood printed glory. They bring the book into their high-rise apartment and soon thereafter their mother, Ellie, becomes possessed by evil and sets about violently attacking them and their neighbors. Aside from the three children trying to survive the other main lead is Ellie's sister Beth portrayed by Lily Sullivan. Beth is there for a family reunion and some sisterly advice involving life choices. The evil hits the fan though before they can really get into and start picking apart and solving their drama.

    The opening of the movie does not take place in the city but instead at a lakeside retreat. An A-frame cabin is shown in one neat establishing shot and it looked like a whimsical place to perhaps vacation. Three people are in the opening: a woman who is possessed by evil, her boyfriend, and her cousin. The possessed woman scalps her cousin with a violent hair rip, mutilates her own face with the blades of a drone, and then throws herself into the lake. Her boyfriend is mauled and decapitated when he jumps into the water after her. Then the possessed woman levitates out of the water and the title of the movie is shown. It is a cool title shot indeed.

    The bulk of the movie ends up taking place in an apartment building and it is not until the very end that things circle around to explain the opening scenes. The woman in the opening happens to live in the building and was oblivious to the horrors that went on in the night and as she is going to her car she is possessed by the evil entity that gave the lead cast so much trouble. It is an almost cute way to bring things around, yet also just fairly random unless the next sequel follows that character and takes place at the lake.

Evil Dead Rise features a lot of blood and lots of solid horror visuals. I enjoyed seeing the antics of Ellie and actually wished for even more scenes with the actor and character. Even acknowledging the consist visual smorgasbord offered by the film I still must say I was never struck with any specific "wow" moment overall.

Prior to this viewing I had heard of a cheese grater being used in a painful fashion. When the moment came I did not feel the hype was warranted. It makes me squeamish to think about a cheese grater being used against someone's flesh and that indeed plays out with Beth getting the back of her leg grated; however, it was not a prolonged sort of attack. I think if the grater had not just torn across her once but had shredded her flesh at least a second time it would have been more gruesome and impactful a scene. The gore overall was not anything I have not really seen before.

Near the end of the movie a few people morph together to make a morbid chimera sort of human/creature to chase after Beth and the little girl Kassie. Perhaps this visual will amaze some horror fans but I immediately just thought of the way a mother and her child were morphed together in the Nicolas Cage starring 2019 film *Color Out of Space*. I thought the usage of that sort of human meld was creepier in the Cage film.

At one point all the dead and possessed people in the movie tell Beth and Kassie that they will be "dead by dawn." They chant those words over and over again. *Dead by Dawn* was a subtitle for *Evil Dead II*. *Dead by Dawn* also happens to be the title of a 2020 film that I wrote the screenplay for.

The *Evil Dead* film series is known for the character

Ash as portrayed by Bruce Campbell. The actor and character are not seen in *Evil Dead Rise*; however, there are some records played in the film giving information via a priest who discovered the *Book of the Dead* and Bruce Campbell's voice can be heard on one of the recordings warning the priest against experimenting with the book.

It is also said that Bruce Campbell provided a sound effect for this movie. There is a scene where Ellie bites out someone's eyeball and the sound effects is Bruce Campbell crunching on an apple. Ellie spits this eyeball out down the hall and it goes into a teenager's open mouth and I guess he chokes to death on it for some reason. The eyeball spitting thing ,while it gets a point for being quirky, was also one of the dumber moments for me in the film.

Evil Dead Rise relies more on horror visuals than it does solid story. I actually found myself often wondering what the "rules" for the events taking place were regarding possession and powers in play. In the end I did not understand at all how the two survivors were not possessed when everyone else was. Outside of possession there are supernatural happenings in the building with blood filling an elevator and wires being animated to grab someone. The odds were against anyone getting out alive and I did not feel like the characters who do did anything to beat those odds — they are just let go in order to have some survivors or heroes.

Beth and Kassie become absolutely drenched in blood in this movie. I enjoy good blood drenching visuals but it's been done in many movies before and *Evil Dead Rise* did not really elevate the usage of such visuals in any way. There is a comfort food feel to how things were handled and *Evil Dead* fans get their blood and even some chainsaw action, but this is a movie to me that the more I think about it afterward the more I question the value overall and want to pick at the elements that formed it. Ultimately, I think leaning more on some intriguing story and original additions would have been better than just visuals. I guess the sheer volume of blood is impressive if comparing gallons to other productions.

3. PEARL - 2022

The movie *Pearl* did not feature anything unexpected in story content but is a cake that I saw through the glass and knew that I wanted. It tasted as imagined with some sweet surprises regarding production value and character depth to tickle the fancies of my gray matter.

Pearl is a prequel to the Ti West written and directed film *X*. He also wrote and directed this film but this time the lead actor Mia Goth also is given writing credit. The material in the movie is backstory for one of the characters that Goth played in *X* and sounds like it started out to better inform her acting motivations for that film rather than seeking to become another complete film. The story studies the character of the title in 1918 as she suffers on the family farm, left behind by her husband who has gone off to war, stuck with her strict mother and invalid father, she does her chores and wishes for more in life. One specific wish is her desire to become a dancer and entertainer. It is evident that Pearl is touched with some madness and, while her demented choices might not be actions that the average viewer can say they support, I think her struggles with the weights of stress and living a life not of her choosing are easy to identify with. "We all go a little mad sometimes," and depending on how mad and how affected the ego the issues that arise or that we cause may need outside of the box solutions to set things "right" again.

There aren't many who will admit that they are capable of the things that Pearl gets up to but maybe if we explore the method within the madness of her decision making we can see the scary reflection of truth.

She kills a goose with a pitchfork and then feeds it to an alligator. Maybe Pearl plays favorites among the animals and the goose rubbed her the wrong way but this murder can also be chalked up to a circle of life: nature is an animal eat animal ordeal and the alligator in the pond needs to eat. She has affection for the gator which she has named Theda after the silent film actress Theda Bara; therefore, why wouldn't she want the creature to have some goose for dinner? Theda is quite the handy friend to have on hand when it comes to hiding crimes in which humans are reduced to meat.

Pearl gets up to some rebellious actions that probably mirror the basic transgressions of most normal youths; going to watch a moving picture show when she is supposed to be running an errand and even taking a drink out of her father's morphine while watching said show; classic kid's stuff. Well, maybe morphine is a bit harder than the drugs the average youth experiments with. But then she gets caught up in a daydream and finds a dance partner in a scarecrow in a corn field and the scene strikes some as creepy behavior. More or less the creepiness depends on how grotesque one finds the scarecrow in the looks department. One might argue that the fact that Pearl ends up riding the scarecrow in a sexual manner is what makes things creepy but if you perverts are being honest you know a lustful act with an inanimate object is not unusual behavior for a human being. Sexual arousal does not fit inside the lines of any rules regardless of whether or not society states otherwise and everyone plays pretend. In the movie *American Pie,* a boy has relations with a pie and Pearl with the scarecrow is no different in a basic sense.

    Pearl gets into a confrontation with her overbearing mother and the fight ends with her mother catching on fire. The introduction of flames to parent were not exactly a thoughtful action and afterward the dragging of her burnt mother to the basement can possibly be seen as an action of panic with a touch of shame. In a sense this event pushes Pearl toward having the guts to commit more heinous acts, sort of like a serial killer who has their first kill fall into their lap in a spur of the moment decision, crime of opportunity moment; however, she technically seek to kill her mother. She does leave her to suffer in extreme pain in the basement and one could say that this is sadistic punishment being doled out but I think her later interactions with her dying mother display that Pearl was scared and confused in the moment when her mother went up in flames.

    When Pearl has sex with the projectionist at the movie theater it is not a mystery as to her motivations—the man speaks the right words and has seduced her into thinking he might take her away, that they might travel and see the world together. Later when he visits her house and she can tell that he senses something is amiss with her she brutally kills him because she knows that he is a liar. She feels betrayed and lashes out perhaps in part due to her own guilt in having slept with the man when she is a married woman. I am not saying that his murder is justified but it is easy to connect the dots as to why she thought he deserved to be executed.

Next she kills her invalid father. It is not done to ease his life of suffering but because she plans to leave the farm and no one will be around to take care of him. It is equal parts the fact that he is a negative weight on her dreams and she does not want him to suffer even worse. A sane person might have sought out care for the man from an outside the family source or charity but Pearl is beyond sane thoughts when she has her burnt mother in the basement already and has fed a lover to the alligator. Later in the movie she expresses regret over having killed her father showing that within the mental struggles and murderous feats there is both conscience and heart within the mix of the woman. She is not an emotionless psycho by any means. Her tears are real.

Pearl chops up her friend and sister-in-law Mitsy with an axe. She does this after Mitsy convinces her to confide her feelings to her. Afterward Pearl senses that Mitsy is disturbed by her words and she does not trust that the woman is not going to reveal her madness to the rest of the world. Again, she is covering her butt regarding being found out for her dark thoughts. We all have dark thoughts that would not go over well with the public at large even if the rest of the public at large are having similar thoughts. Therefore, while the steps she takes to keep her secret feelings secret are extreme the basic motivation there is understandable. Also, one cannot overlook that this murder might involve a touch of jealousy as well for she suspects her friend got the dancing job that she herself wished to nail down.

In the end the inner struggles come to a head and Pearl is aware that she has been doing "wrong" and attempts to clean up her crimes to present a normal face and household, but the human mind can only be twisted so far before it breaks and as the end credits roll the breakdown is evident, if it wasn't already when she is shown distraught about not being chosen for the dance troupe after her audition. Mental turmoil is a human condition that everyone will face at some point if not daily and while Pearl's crimes are disgusting by the standards of society when it comes to the laws of nature, well, you haven't seen enough nature documentaries if you think they are playing nice in the wilderness.

This film has retro flair with the style in which Ti West chose to shoot it. The entire movie feels like you have been dropped into the same world in which *The Wizard of Oz* takes place. Instead of a young girl wishing to get back home from her amazing adventure you have a woman willing to kill to escape from home in order to go on an adventure.

Mia Goth stars as Pearl and she also donned a lot of makeup to play the older version of herself in the movie *X*. In *X* she had dual roles being the younger actor Maxine who might be a character who returns in yet another film in what I understand is a burgeoning franchise of fun madness. Considering how quickly the first two films came together I reckon a third might already be out as you read this.

Mia Goth is English, born in Southwark, London, England in 1993 on October the 25th. As of this writing she is romantically linked in Hollywood to Shia LaBeouf and gave birth to their daughter in the same year that saw the releases of *Pearl* and *X*. In theory LaBeouf and Goth make for an interesting couple if one thinks of the industry that they work within and their creative talents.

They met on the set of the 2012 film *Nymphomaniac* in 2012.

In *Pearl* and as Pearl, Mia Goth puts in a splendid performance. She is creepy in how far she is willing to go to reach for her dreams. She puts a human face on the imperfect balance that is selfishness and ambition while also being a believable monster born from a mind incapable of navigating those waters with sanity. My favorite sections of the movie are a long monologue that she delivers near the end, a journey of words that had me hanging on her every emotion and thought expressed. And then the shot used to end the movie and held into the credits—Mia Goth gives an exaggerated smile to the camera and holds it, wide, and too long. The smile looks painful and eventually tears do fall from her eyes and it is a beautiful end cap of what the movie was as it looks like she could break into mad laughter but then bawl. The acting performance by Mia Goth argues that genre films deserve more attention when it comes to mainstream movie awards.

4. X - 2022

The movie *X* is to *The Texas Chain Saw Massacre* what its prequel *Pearl* is to *The Wizard of Oz*. It borrows style elements but the story material doesn't totally fit the mold regarding what our eyes tell us should be happening due to the familiar visuals; I think Pearl did a more interesting job at this but X was the staging grounds for the thought process and working out ideas probably because it was shot first. Writer and director Ti West seems to be having fun and engaging himself with a creative challenge regarding this series of films and it sounds like a happy place to be in as an artist—I hope to reap more rewards as a viewer with more connected films. The movie studios are all about creating franchises based on "universes" thanks to the booming success of interconnected Marvel comic book movies and one based around fame hungry killers: why not?

X follows a group of folks in 1979 as they seek fame and fortune by shooting their own pornographic film. The location they choose to shoot their movie in is the same farm from the move *Pearl*. If you watch the movies in chronological order instead of the order in which they were released then you know about the bloodshed that already occurred at said farm in the early 1900s. Pearl from the first film is still kicking around the grounds with her husband Howard, only now her demented bloodlust is not just fueled by dreams of making it big as a dancer, rather she is haunted by the pain of "what could have been" and an inner rage over the passing of time, the aging process, and seeing younger folks poised to catch their dreams when she failed to ever leave the farm. Pearl and Howard kill their visitors one by one.

    The film is a slasher horror movie and pays homage to 70s film *The Texas Chain Saw Massacre* in setting but it really moves at its own pace which is to say more like an Indie relationship drama. It is a very slow movie and while I have enjoyed it both times that I have seen it the second time did drag a tad more. The same moments of emotional impact that were helped by the pacing, however, remain as deep on repeated viewing. One can really feel the weight of Pearl's lifetime of longing.

    Mia Goth portrays Pearl hidden underneath aging makeup. On my first viewing of *X* I suspected that the elderly folks were not real elderly actors but I had no idea that Pearl was Mia Goth. She takes on dual roles in this film also being the actor in the group that like Pearl has a strong desire for fame and is told by others that she has the "x factor." She wants to be special really bad and Pearl recognizes herself within it. These movies showcase Mia Goth's acting skills in a way that should generate a decent helping of fans willing to follow her from project to project to get more, to see what she does next.

    The ringleader of the filmmaking group is Wayne and he is portrayed by Martin Henderson. He is a New Zealand born actor whom I am not all that familiar with; however, I can imagine that people mistake him for Luke Wilson. The movie was shot in his birth country of New Zealand.

    Brittany Snow plays the porn actor Bobby-Lynn

and her male co-star is Jackson portrayed by Kid Cudi. Kid Cudi is the stage name for musical artist Scott Ramon Seguro Mescudi. The film crew for the group is a boyfriend/girlfriend team, Lorraine and RJ, whose relationship ends up on shaky grounds providing some drama for the film. This couple is portrayed by Jenna Ortega and Owen Campbell. While Mia Goth ends up being "the final girl" and the star of these movies, Jenna Ortega's face demonstrating horror was used in some key promotional art for *X*. The movie *Pearl* ends with Mia Goth holding a crazy smile and in *X* I think Jenna Ortega portraying fear when she discovers a hanging corpse in the basement of the farmhouse is an impressive expression as well. Ortega is blessed with large eyes that do well conveying emotion on camera.

  RJ is the first to die in the movie and it is the death scene that sets *X* apart from other slasher films to some degree. Pearl stabs him in the throat but once is not enough, she straddles him and stabs him in the neck over and over again with the mutilation shown on screen. After the bloody business Pearl then stands up and does a little dance in the spotlight provided by the headlights of RJ's vehicle. The song *Oui, Oui, Marie* by goth rocker Chelsea Wolfe kicks on and really stamps the moment into memory. *X* takes the viewer to an emotional depth not present in most slasher features.

  Aside from being a little slow at times the other downside to *X* in my opinion is that many scenes are too dark and blurry. The movie *Pearl* may have been a simple and somewhat predictable story regarding character exploration but I think it looked like a million bucks compared to *X* and thus more intriguing to watch visually. Even the slasher *The Texas Chain Saw Massacre* in my memory is more vivid to behold than this film claiming it as an inspiration. There is something really special about the atmospheric tone of the original *Texas Chain Saw Massacre* and *X* does not manage to emulate that "x factor" at all.

    The porno that the characters are shooting is about a man coming across some sexually charged farmer's daughters. There is a real 1976 pornographic film titled *Farmer's Daughters*. I have never seen that adult flick but it sounds like the version being shot in *X* is tame compared to the Zebedy Colt directed and starred in one that has a synopsis describing a mad series of rapes and incest as the plot.

    X is a fun movie if you are in the mood for a genre piece with emotional depth; you get a classic genre scenario and setting with nudity aplenty as well. I think the actors all had great presence and even if I got frustrated trying to fiddle with the sound and picture lighting for some scenes, the movie has strong moments with enough impact that I will be able to access them quickly in the filing cabinet of movie memories in my brain.

5. MEN - 2022

Men was written and directed by Alex Garland who really grabbed a lot of attention with his film *Ex Machina*. He followed up that movie with the Natalie Portman starring *Annihilation* which I have also seen but really cannot recall the content well enough to describe or assign meaning. *Men* is another "thinker" of a film with an artistic approach rather than a commercial one and I am not sure that all the critical dissections I have seen of the film are regarding "what does it mean." I don't think it left me caring what the deeper meaning might have been if there was one. THAT sounds negative but I actually enjoyed the film.

Jessie Buckley stars in the film as Harper. An Irish singer and actress, Buckley first and foremost to me is Oraetta Mayflower from the fourth season of the television show *Fargo*. She was magnificent in *Fargo* and the demented character really stood out all the way until her ending. As I see her in more projects outside of *Fargo* I wager Oraetta might just be one of many performances I find memorable because she is someone with interesting screen presence overall with the creative magic of quirk in her smiles, eyes, and voice.

The story features Harper on a countryside vacation after her husband, whom she was in the midst of leaving, died via either accident or suicide. One can say that the film is exploring themes of guilt and toxic masculinity, but the way it does this might be lost on many in the audience because it has Harper visiting a countryside town where all the men seem to have variations of the same face and start to stalk and frighten her at the place she is staying. Rory Kinnear puts in the performance as the men, an odd but effective one from man to man.

    The locations and scenery in this film are astounding. There are a lot of camera shots that linger on the sights and sounds of the greenery and while this might make things move slow for a viewer depending on their mood I enjoyed the imagery. There is some artwork at a church that I have read are well known images in England. One is of the Green Man and the other sheela na gig. When the camera explores the sculptures at the church I could not help but think about the Irish horror movie *Rawhead Rex* and the fertility themes within it. *Men* was shot in the United Kingdom.

    Men works gore into the story in an intense and raw feeling way. The aftermath of Harper's husband falling or jumping from an upper floor of their building and landing half impaled on a fence was disturbing. One of Harper's nude male stalkers takes his cures from the Green Man art symbol and slices his face open to plant greenery into the openings. An arm reaching through a mail slot gets stabbed and then retracts, dragging and cutting the blade through the length of the limb and splitting the hand. This split hand is used by the men with disturbing effect later on, specifically when the Vicar character reaches up and holds on to Harper with the mangled appendage. And then you have: the birthing scene.

    The finale of *Men* features a man shambling after

Harper who pulls up short and in pain, goes to the ground and a vagina appears below his testicles. He births one of the other men from the story who gets up and continues the chase only to also stop to give birth to another man, who then gives birth to another man, and what you get is one of the weirdest horror chase sequences of all time with men birthing men in pursuit of the woman. The final man born is Harper's dead husband who is portrayed by Papa Essiedu. How and why? What does it all mean? I find myself not actually caring.

I have read people who interpret the ending of *Men* to symbolize this or that and when the men start birthing out of one another it is all just Harper having a psychotic break or manifesting the incident. I choose not to believe in that interpretation because that is too easy an explanation. I prefer to see the incident as having really happened as seen, the men were birthing men, and the fact is I do not need a logical explanation. It is far more wondrous and delightfully horrible to accept it as IT HAPPENED!

Men is a thinker movie where I found myself turning off my thinker and embracing the images, performances, and story as a witness not trying to decipher any meaning beyond "it is what it is." I thought it was interesting and entertaining to behold though I do not see it as something I will be compelled to return to in a repeat fashion. I will see the artwork of the film and always remember: that's that men birthing men movie starring the killer nurse from *Fargo*.

6. THE MUMMY - 2017

    Tom Cruise movies are usually guaranteed success at the box office; however, the 2017 horror action flick *The Mummy* flopped hard enough that the movie studio canceled the entire universe of movies they had planned to spin off of it. The idea was to copy the Marvel superhero formula of interconnected characters weaving in and out of each other's movies only to do so with the classic monsters of Universal Studios fame such as the mummy, the wolf man, Dracula, Frankenstein related characters, and the Creature from the Black Lagoon. This was to be called the Dark Universe. I have read some behind the scenes quotes from people who claim they knew the Dark Universe was doomed before *The Mummy* even began filming. This person paints a picture of the creative meetings as being a bunch of people with a bunch of ideas but no solid ideas on how to actually execute a singular vision for weaving the Dark Universe together. Too many cooks in the kitchen and Tom Cruise is a movie star of epic proportions, clout not height, and I bet he got right into the mix flinging his sauce around.
    Alex Kurtzman was known more as writer and producer than a director before he landed this high-profile gig. His only feature film directing credit prior to this was the 2012 Chris Pine starring drama *People Like Us*. It is said that Len Wiseman, who is known for the *Underworld* vampire action series of films, was the original directing choice. However, over time, with all the fingers

poking into the pie, Wisemen retracted his own and did not have any mummy finger pie.

Tom Cruise stars as Nick Morton, a soldier who along with his pal Vail, portrayed by Jake Johnson, likes to hunt relics to sell on the black market. Their latest hunt involves some information he borrowed from Jenny Halsey, portrayed by Annabel Wallis, and long tomb discovering story short they end up finding the mummy of a cursed woman that once upon a time made a deal with the powers of evil due to her being jealous over never going to get the power ton rule Egypt. She murders her family and then attempts to bring the evil entity known as Set into the body of a human man before she is stopped and imprisoned. The mummy gets out of her prison and sets out to finish what she started with the desire to put Set into Morton's body. Sofia Boutella portrays Ahmanet the mummy. Russell Crowe is another key cast member as Henry Jekyll. Jenny Halsey works for Jekyll to stop the evils of the world, a passion project of his considering he is indeed the Jekyll of Doctor Jekyll and Mr. Hyde fame afflicted with some evil himself.

When Nick Morton is introduced as a character he is a complete jerk. I understand that his selfishness is meant to be a part of his character arc but, even though Cruise tries to make him carefree and playful, I found him too next level jerk to ever root for. He wants to get an artifact out of an area that is crawling with murderous terrorists, a risk that his friend Vail does not wish to take. However, Morton forces him to go along with him by destroying the man's water canteen, a death sentence considering they are traveling in the vast desert. Vail and Nick go down into the town and right away the bullets start flying. They run around some but it really does look like they will be killed for a moment and it is all played like these are the usual hijinks Nick pulls on his pal Vail, but literally he is a bully to Vail and signing him up to die. Of course, they end up surviving. Well, for a bit. Once they are investigating the tomb they uncover, Vail gets bitten by a spider that turns him into an undead joke, similar to the zombies in *An America Werewolf in London*.

    The imbalance of vision and tone approach is evident in the way this movie plays out. It has tentpole action sequences, darker horror elements, and then juvenile dialog with Morton obsessed with the fact that Halsey claims he only lasted 15 seconds when doing the sexy time with her. I have read some people stating that *The Mummy* failed because he lacked the element of "fun," however, I am not sure that is exactly it. I actually think that the attempts to put "fun" into the movie helped doom it. Personally, I wish they had leaned harder into the serious horror elements in play and went DARK DARK UNIVERSE. An action horror movie can have some natural humor to fall into but it feels too forced here and does not land, with that criticism mostly being centered on Tom Cruise and his character, since he is at the center of the movie. A thought: it is called *The Mummy*, maybe make the mummy the main character?

    I liked Sofia Boutella as Ahmanet. She managed to bring sexiness to the crustiness of having been mummified. Visually her character is really cool and her drive to bring evil into the world is interesting enough. They paint her over with a lot of CGI it seems like to me and it left me wondering: why couldn't they have just featured more of the actor in makeup?

Most of the acting performances aside from Boutella's presence are run-of-the-mill, making people dull props amongst special effects shots. Russell Crowe as Jekyll is basically another version of the comic book character the Hulk. I think there were plans to give the character his own spinoff film, but the comic book superpowers approach would have made that one dumb film, I think.

In the quest to stop the evil that is Set, Henry Jekyll's grand plan is to let Nick be possessed by him and then in that form the evil he predicts will be more vulnerable and can be destroyed. So, to stop the mummy's evil plan they plan to let the plan go through? Only without letting the mummy lady do it herself, they'll just chain her up to watch? When Nick finds out about this plan he is not into it. It is odd to me that the plan is to kill him but once they have him as a captive, they just let him walk around and hang out waiting to spring the plot onto him later. Why not just keep Nick tied up like the mummy so he can't escape?

In the end battle Jenny Halsey is mortally wounded and Nick ends up letting himself get possessed by Set so that he can wield the powers of evil for the sake of goodness. He defeats Ahmanet by sucking out her life-force, a trick she has been pulling on people making herself a dehydrated looking zombie army, and then resurrects Jenny. He also resurrects his buddy Vail, and the end of the movie has them in the desert again seeking answers to the curse of powers that Nick now possesses. I am not sure what he is supposed to be now that he is part Set and part Nick, Super Devil Man? It sounds similar in construct to what the Jekyll has got going on.

I can see some good ideas regarding the horror elements in play within *The Mummy*. The action set pieces are solid and overall this bazillion dollar movie looks like a bazillion bucks. There is no reason it couldn't have been more entertaining. I think they actually came close to pulling it off but in trying to be all things to everybody it failed to find its identity.

7. LIFEFORCE – 1985

The 1976 novel *The Space Vampires* served as the inspiration for the film *Lifeforce* which at one point shared the title of the book before transitioning to the new one which is based off of what the vampire drain out of a person. Directed by Tobe Hooper, *The Texas Chain Saw Massacre* and *Poltergeist* director, *Lifeforce* is said to have been a miserable flop as a film upon release but one that later gained a "cult" following. A trio of vampires are discovered inter space and then brought back to Earth where they proceed to drain people of energy and leap into their minds. I think the premise is fun enough but that the cult following has got to be people tuning into ogle the lead nude vampire woman.

Right away: reboot candidate. There are some fun concepts in *Lifeforce* and I thought it was really cool how their spacecraft was discovered hiding in the tail of Halley's Comet. The ship and the exploration of it by the astronauts attempts to be epic in scope, but the special effects are not very realistic and when paired with the loud, sweeping orchestral music the moments played more cheesy than not.

When I think back to this movie I recall bat creatures discovered, nude vampires, space exploration, a comet, mayhem in the streets as people are turned into feral vampires, and it sounds like it was an exciting movie. However, the bulk of the movie is a bunch of men in suits taking about the problem of having vampires on

Earth causing trouble. It is all a very dull exercise in the bureaucratic process behind an apocalyptic emergency.

After a vampire sucks the life out of a victim, that person shrivels up and appears dead for a couple of hours. However, they then become animated and hunger to suck the life out of another person. The undead people are not very realistic regarding the puppetry and special effects. They reminded me somewhat of worse versions of Tarman from *Return of the Living Dead*. The visual style of these effects works well for the zany fun that was *Return of the Living Dead* but do nothing to make the stuffy atmosphere of *Lifeforce* crackle.

A young Mathilda May stars as the main vampire in *Lifeforce*. She walks around in the film completely nude and she is quite a fetching, striking, sensual visual to behold. A French born actress I have read that she did not even speak English when cast into the role but rather got the part due to her comfort with being in the buff. It has also been written that director Tobe Hooper was fairly obsessed with making sure May's nude form was presented just right in the feature. Specifically, there was a lot of back and forth shaving and shaping of pubic hair that became somewhat controversial in the minds of some. Anyway, look up and look her in the eyes because I think a lot of her performance in the film comes from those windows to the soul and she did a solid job as a soul sucking nudist.

I did want to take the movie serious and the nude vampire imagery as serious art not smut but then there was a shot of May's breast as a shadow on the wall and my brain went into Beavis and Butthead mode: "Huh. Huh. Shadow boob." I reiterate though Mathilda May does a solid job off having "presence" in the film and when she stalks out of the building over glass exploded from doors and windows it makes for a solid audition to be a killer in a *Terminator* film.

Revered actor Patrick Stewart arrives late in the film as Dr. Armstrong. It turns out that this doc running an asylum actually has the vampire woman inside his head controlling him. It gets freaky with Patrick Stewart getting himself a scene in which he is drugged and while lying on a table emits a deep lady voice telling a dude that he/she loves him. After some slaps and yelling Patrick Stewart and the fella play smoochy face. Okay, maybe it is not the nude vampire but rather Patrick Stewart that makes *Lifeforce* a "cult classic."

The guy kissing Patrick Stewart is Steve Railsback playing the role of Carlsen. When the spacecraft returns to Earth the entire crew is dead in what felt to me like a nod to the Dementer ship from *Dracula*. Carlsen did not perish, however, and ejected himself in an escape pod. The men on Earth just chalk him up as "missing" for a while but then later his escape pod lands on Earth. The logistics of how he arrives on Earth much later were lost on me.

At one point they say that the vampire beings have been to Earth before, having ridden the comet, and that the vampire legends of old sprouted from them. However, they later state that the vampires need to learn about humans as hosts which implies that they are not familiar with humans from previous visits. I found that lore development a little confusing.

The ending showdown of the movie disappointed me. The lights of "lifeforce" flying about and the chaos in the streets seem like someone at least saved a little money for these sections—I have read that there were a lot of financial issues during the movie shoot. There wasn't a true conclusion though regarding "is it over?" *Lifeforce* has a lot of cool elements but they did not pump enough life into the production as executed. I really think this material could be revised and made far more exciting with a lot more vampire action and better special effects.

8. INFINITY POOL – 2023

The writer and director of *Infinity Pool* comes from a Hollywood lineage by way of Canada being the son of famed director David Cronenberg; *The Fly*, *Videodrome*, *A History of Violence*. Brandon Cronenberg seems happy to keep the spirit of his father's work alive within his own projects the familial influence seeming obvious to me regarding outside of the box, weird edginess being present in his films. *Infinity Pool* isn't a movie that cares about letting you get comfortable with what you are witnessing and does not seek to sell popcorn to a mainstream audience.

The premise for *Infinity Pool* is that a struggling book author and his wife go to a vacation resort in order for him to seek inspiration for his writing career. The resort is in a unique and impoverished country and leaving the confines of the resort is frowned upon. Of course, James and his wife Em, venture out beyond the fences after meeting and being persuaded to do so by another couple: Gabi and Alban. During their excursion James accidentally runs over a native citizen of the nation and discovers that there are harsh punishments even for an accident: he is sentenced to death. It is in this predicament, facing execution, that science fiction twists into the story with James being informed that for a price he can have a double made of himself to be killed in his place. The cost of having yourself copied and killed goes beyond financial as James becomes more and more fascinated with the process and the new friends he has made through experiencing it.

    Alexander Skarsgård portrays author James Foster and his wife is Em Foster portrayed by Cleopatra Coleman. There are several actors who portray the group of tourists who push James into doing naughty deeds but the main center of focus regarding them is Gabi, portrayed by Mia Goth. I think Mia Goth brought the most attention to this project coming off of her strong performances in *X* and *Pearl*. I think that all the actors do a solid job in their roles and help the unsettling nature of the story along; they fit within the creeping creepiness.

    The premise of the movie is an interesting one and the exploration of crime and punishment, morals and selfishness are all "thinker" elements put into play as you see people embarking on sinful adventures without consequences. However, when it comes to the involvement of clones and the repeated execution of them, I felt like the obvious angle to steal a lot of the attention regarding it being a "thinker' piece of entertainment—a question brought up by the characters themselves at one point— is whether or not the person you are watching is the original, or are they the clone having replaced them? In that regard, even if you are confused by how the film plays out, it is still somewhat "predictable."

    While I did not find *Infinity Pool* to be a totally stimulating experience I did like the depth and depravity of the character studies. The lead actors brought their characters to life and they felt corrupted and dirty; Mia Goth in the later portions pushes villainy with her sometimes unhinged feeling of actor energy and success in making you despise the character in those moments. Horrible people doing horrible things though may not be enough for some if they find the "thinker" elements not too fresh.

In the end the diabolical characters transform into "normal" people as they are heading back to the "real" world once the vacation is over. I found these scenes far more scary and interesting than any of the bloodletting and gory butchering that proceeded them.

9. DEMON KNIGHT - 1995

The official title for this movie is *Tales from the Crypt: Demon Knight* and was the first in a planned film series spinning off the television show *Tales from the Crypt* which itself was a spinoff of the comic book series from EC Comics. And in a weird turn of events, as a kid I did not care for *Demon Knight* the movie because I read the book *Demon Knight* authored by Randall Boyll first. The book is touted as a novelization based on the screenplay for the movie. The screenplay was not based on an old EC comic but was an original tale converted after passing through the hands of different producers and directors as a standalone horror project. I have not read the book since I was that 90s kid but still in my mind the content of it is superior to the film. However, the film is not that bad either.

"Fasten your drool cups and hold on to your vomit bags. We're going to the movies."

Ernest R. Dickerson directed *Demon Knight,* with a plot in which a guy named Brayker is on the run from The Collector because he has an ancient key with the power to keep demons from returning darkness to the Earth. Brayker ends up hiding out at a church converted into a motel in Wormwood, New Mexico. He and the residents of the motel try to survive the night as The Collector and the demons he summons try to get inside. Other movies directed by Dickerson include: *Juice, Surviving the Game, Bulletproof,* and *Bones*. He has also directed a lot of television show episodes for popular properties such as *Dexter, House of Cards,* and *The Walking Dead.*

The movie opens up with a short horror clip that serves no purpose other than to have a scream queen show off her boobs and screaming abilities. It also features puns and a cameo by actor John Larroquette. I feel like there was an opening short in the book as well but one that had more going on regarding a woman having murdered her husband tale. My guess is that the movie production took a lot of budget short cuts and just went for setting a B movie tone. The actual meat of the feature balances in more serious moments than one might expect with the campiness.

In the opening section when the Crypt Keeper is on set directing a movie he is shown to run around. This special effect does not play well. Visually the Crypt Keeper standing in one place as a puppet is far more effective. The voice of the Crypt Keeper is John Kassir.

The opening credits and shots of the movie start off right in the music department with the rock song *Hey Man Nice Shot* by the band Filter playing. The music soundtrack did rank within the top 200 on the Billboard charts with acts such as Pantera, Ministry, Machine Head, Megadeth, Melvins, Rollins Band, Biohazard, Sepultura, and Gravediggaz contributing. Personally, the Filter track is the best out of the bunch and an iconic song for a rock fan overall.

William Sadler stars as Brayker and he is being pursued by The Collector portrayed by Billy Zane. The cast of characters who get trapped in the motel include actors Jada Pickett Smith, Brenda Bakke, CCH Pounder, Dick Miller, Charles Fleischer, and Thomas Haden

Church. All of the actors tackled their assignments well, I believe—good performances all across the board. If one had to pick a standout the inclination is to lean toward Bill Zane as the villain just because he gets to ham it up some and provide "fun" with the horror. Appearing as a Party Babe in a fantasy sequence is adult film star Chasey Lain but she is not the only notable name featured in the fantasy with Traci Bingham making her feature film debut as a Party Babe as well. Bingham would go on to television fame as the character Jordan Tate on *Baywatch*.

There is a scene where the character Cordelia, a prostitute portrayed by Brenda Bakke, lounges on a table as she tries to seduce Brayker into perhaps buying what she sells. A cat jumps onto the table and the CCH Pounder character, Irene, exclaims, "Get that pussy off the table." Cordelia hops off the table quickly and Irene proceeds to explain the punchline of the joke by stating: "I meant the cat." It is still a funny joke but I think it would have been far more memorable and hilarious to me if Cordelia had jumped off the table as the visual punchline without Irene having to clarify what just transpired.

When the demons first appear in the movie it seems like they should have and could have taken over and ended things right away. However, these entities kind of pose and lumber around slowly more than not. They do not come across very threatening in my opinion but they do look kind of cool, sort of looking like the Crypt Keeper made some babies with the trolls from the *Lord of the Rings* movies.

Charles Fleischer is the character Wally in the film. He is a mailman who has been fired, bemoans the accusations that he was reading other people's mail.

Wally gets killed by a demon early on but the other characters find his stash of stolen mail later on and that is another solid joke. Even better if you can appreciate the darkest of jokes: they find his stash of guns and realize that he was plotting to go "postal." I think the fact that he is shown as such a sad sack and sympathetic character while alive is why these revelations are hilarious.

The character Irene gets her arm ripped off in a bloody scene but survives. The fact that she goes around with one arm missing and like nothing happened for the rest of her time in the film might annoy you or maybe you salute it as a B movie aspect helping keep the more serious moments from dragging down the energy of the production.

Honestly, *Demon Knight* does not have crackling energy for me overall. There is fun and it is well acted and directed, but the pacing was not keeping me on the edge of my seat. I like the movie better than younger me but at the same time it is one that I can easily walk away from at any given time and not feel like I am missing out. I do think the story presents enough in the form of characters and scenarios that sequels taking place afterward or even tales from the past involving The Collector would be worthy explorations.

10. FIVE NIGHTS AT FREDDY'S - 2023

Five Nights at Freddy's is a movie directed by Emma Tammi based off the popular video game series that I personally have never played. Before watching this movie my awareness of the property was only vague regarding being familiar with the name and having seen associated art on different products for the brand. There are a lot of writers with credit for the screenplay, including the director Tammi, but fans of the source material probably like to see that Scott Cawthon, the creator of the video game, was involved.

Josh Hutcherson stars as the lead, Mike, who takes an overnight security job at an out of business pizza joint that has animatronic animals inside. The animatronics come to life and it seems like they are not opposed to killing people which is just the tip of the iceberg when it comes to the haunted past of the establishment and some kids who went missing. Matthew Lillard, Piper Rubio, Elizabeth Lail, and Mary Stuart Masterson are some of the other actors with major parts.

Josh Hutcherson is an actor that I know by both name and face but for the life of me cannot really remember ever actually seeing him in a movie. After looking up his past works I have of course seen many flicks he has been in but I guess his star making claim to fame is considered *The Hunger Games* films. I've only seen the first film in that series. It's weird to me that you can say his name and I can think: "Yeah, that guy," yet not place his face in an actual movie.

It was a lot of fun seeing Matthew Lillard in this movie. As a fan of his portrayal of Stu in the movie *Scream* seeing him in this horror movie made me think about the possibility of him returning in that other franchise. In the last *Scream* movie that I watched I recall there being a line said about "if Stu is even dead," and even if that line ruins things and makes his return to the franchise predictable I am still all for it. It would be a ton of fun to see older Matthew Lillard tapping into the zaniness of psycho younger Matthew Lillard, err, I mean Stu.

When a horror movie is rated PG-13 I do not come into it expecting to be won over by the horror elements. I think that *Five Nights at Freddy's* does a good job, however, of developing the overall atmosphere right from the start. The opening scene with the security guard being chased and then strapped into a chair to have an animatronic head filled with buzzsaws lowered onto him was an energetic start even if the whimpering and squeaks of fright from the actor were a tad cartoonish.

It is overly critical of me perhaps to call out the opening whimpers of the security guard when later in the movie there is a burly vandal named Hank who screams his head off and I thought that was amusing. The man screaming reminded me of something I wrote once. I wrote a screenplay called *Breath of Hate* that eventually got made into a movie that the distributor titled *The Last House*. When it came to be known to me that Jack Forcinito would be playing the role of Sonny in the movie I tweaked a scene describing him unleashing "scream queen" death screams. Knowing Jack from having worked with him on *Silent Night, Zombie Night* and a subsequent drunken night hanging out in Vegas casino for a festival showing of it, it amused me to try and get him to scream as high-pitched as possible. Ultimately I think Jack was a little too protective of his manly persona on screen and he didn't want to go out like that but Christian Stokes who portrays Hank in *Five Nights at Freddy's* shows us how it should be done.

    Twenty-five minutes into *Five Nights at Freddy's* and my attention was drifting. I think fans of the game probably get more service from this movie than the oblivious but for a good portion of that opening time there is basic setup family drama and some looking around in the dark with a flashlight.

    The custody battle plot with Mike trying to keep his sister Abby, Piper Rubio, at home with him while their aunt Jane, Mary Stuart Masterson, wants to be granted custody is more annoying than not. The lawyer for Aunt Jane as portrayed by Michael P. Sullivan is hilarious with his demeanor, but he and the Aunt both are a better fit for a more slapstick comedy I think. I think it was said that Aunt Jane doesn't care about Abby and just wants custody to get checks from the government and I guess those are lucrative because she is willing to go to some silly means and spend cash to make Mike look like a failure. Her deviousness was too ludicrous.

    One plot set forth by Aunt Jane is to have some hoodlums bust up Freddy's to make Mike lose his security gig. They wait for him to end his shift and then sneak in. It seemed off to me that they want Mike to lose his job as a security guard but his shift is over when they attack the place. I guess him getting blamed for not locking up is the angle but it felt like a stretch to me in plotting. The scenario does give the movie the most interesting horror kills, however, as the animatronics come to life to punish the intruders.

The animatronics are brought to life by Jim Henson Company puppeteers and people wearing the actual suits. They are really cool and interesting I think, but for the most part I felt like them as horror entities lacked scenes of action aside from the taking care of the intruders. They stomp about some and eyeball people a lot but I never felt like the energy level for the movie was pumped up high enough for me.

The ending of the movie has the main antagonist in his "defeat" say the line "I always come back." This went over my head, no clue what he meant by that and I also could not figure out why the lighting fixtures of the place started falling. It was a classic, "the place is collapsing and we gotta get out of here" movie moment, except, the place didn't really collapse and the animatronics are shown to still be hanging out in there afterward.

The movie looks great, well shot, loved the way the sky is captured when Mike and the police officer Vanessa sit outside and he tells her about his "issues." The acting is good, the special effects a treat, overall tone and atmosphere: A plus stuff. The plot, however, felt like too much attempted and none of it landing. Again, I feel like maybe some stuff was lost on me having not played the video games, but the storytelling here was like, um, let's say the plot points are dots for a connect the dots picture—well, there are a lot of dots and they are all floating around making it hard to connect them to form any meaningful picture. I actually find most video games to have weak storytelling and as a gamer tend to prefer just mindless shooting at things strategy games because of that. *Five Nights at Freddy's* felt like bad video game story writing. The kidnapped brother dreams, the imaginary friends, the ghost children, the animatronics, a lot of puzzle pieces that felt not fitting but forced.

According to the press, *Five Night at Freddy's* is doing really well at the box office as I write this. It must have been a popular video game and I happy for fans getting their hit of nostalgia. The movie did not bring this outsider in and make me a fan of the brand, however.

11. ZOMBIELAND - 2009

If you miss the opening narration bits for *Zombieland* the opening title credits do a good job of letting one know what sort of movie they are in for. You're either in the mood for dumb comedy and dumb violence or you're not. Sure, one can say that there is more to the movie than dumbness, but still, slow motion zombie attacks, including topless zombie strippers, while the Metallica song *For Whom the Bell Tolls* rocks out IS the vibe of *Zombieland*. As I watched and listened I was conflicted, thinking "this is commercial dumbness to the dumbest degree," and "this looks cool."

Zombieland, directed by Ruben Fleischer, stars Jesse Eisenberg, Woody Harrelson, Emma Stone, and Abigail Breslin as characters trying to survive in the America after an outbreak has turned the majority of the population into flesh hungry monsters, AKA zombies. Eisenberg as Columbus is the main character and narrator and I think I am curious as to whether or not I would like a *Zombieland* product better with a different lead. This is not a knock at Eisenberg at all, I just did not find him as paired with the character he had to try and flesh out as being all that compelling or interesting. Then again, why was I trying to be compelled? Bring out the monsters!

I have read that the screenplay for this movie was originally a television concept and this is why the running "rules for survival" and "kill of the aspect" jokes are in there; holdovers from a different format in which they might have played better. I mention those aspects because I didn't actually care for them.

The first and only time I ever saw this movie prior to this watching was when it was released in theaters. I did not realize that Amber Heard was in the movie. However, as I watched the events unfold this time I saw her character and wondered: is that Amber Heard? I still had to look it up to confirm it. She has only a bit part as a neighbor turned zombie, known by her apartment number 406, but I think the performance is one of her stronger ones. Even with her level of fame I am not sure that she has ever gotten a role yet that I would consider "breakout" or amazing and as I write this it seems like the Gods of pop culture may be trying to curse her to be known as the woman who might have pooped on Johnny Depp's bed.

Zombieland is a comedy but it's not one that makes me laugh very much. My first chuckle though came when Woody Harrelson's character, Tallahassee, first meets Columbus. It is a line of dialog that got me: "I'm not easy to get along with and I'm sensing you're a bit of a bitch."

Once the male characters meet up with the female characters the main relationship exploration is a romantic one between Columbus and Emma Stone's character Witchita. I'm not saying it turns into a full-blown romance story but the usual boy pining after a girl, inexperienced man-child/teenager stuff. It did seem odd to me that the extra tough and manly Tallahassee in this end of the world scenario did not actually show any interest in Wichita himself. True, she is much younger than he is, but they are living in rough times and he seems like a man about taking what he wants to some degree and exerting his dominance. I guess he is an inner "soft" guy with a tragic past of having lost his child but it still felt odd that a film with the edginess already presented that the boy/girl politics would be so wholesome in this regard.

There is a scene where the survivor group lets off steam by destroying a gift shop business, smashing displays and flinging products around. The business was one selling Native American themed items and it made me wonder if visually having a group of white people smashing up Native American things was meant to convey some sort of message.

The most memorable aspect of this movie is the Bill Murray cameo as himself. He gets shot and killed because he tries to prank Columbus into thinking he is a zombie. The punchline for this joke starts to linger a little too long, but I think Emma Stone delivers her final line and thoughts on it in an entertaining fashion that cements it as funny and fun. I have read that there were quite a few zombie cameo roles offered to celebrities who did not come to play like Murray did.

When the group arrives at Bill Murray's house there is a scene where Tallahassee jumps onto a bed and Wichita walks by holding a gun. I just want to point out that she is not using proper safety awareness and is pointing the gun at her pal as she walks past him.

While I am saying that the usage of Bill Murray is hilarious, my actual second chuckle during the movie came when Columbus and Tallahassee seem to be parting ways because Columbus wants to go after the women who have left. Columbus is going to drive off all heroic on a motorcycle. He starts the vehicle and drives forward and then right into some bushes and crashes. This simple gag got me.

Wichita and her sister character Little Rock, portrayed by Abigail Breslin, decide to go to a theme park with big rides such as roller coasters. The final action sequences occur in this park as zombies arrive in large groups trying to eat the women and the men arrive to try and rescue them. The action is goofy yet fun, plenty of spectacle to behold. However, a piece of my brain that did not shut off kept wondering how the women were operating the large rides as they got on them. For example, they ride a giant pirate ship shaped thing that swooshes pendulum style up high and back down. How did they shut the ride down and get off again without someone at the controls? Later they work the controls of a ride by shooting them but I'm not sure why they would expect that to work. I would assume shooting a machine would just damage it and not yield any results.

Zombieland is a movie that a part of me wants to claim to dislike. In fact, I was not into it at all the first time I watched it. It was easy enough to get into and allow to entertain me during this watch. Even if I was not laughing at the comedy, the fun factor is there.

12. SLEEPY HOLLOW - 1999

Beheadings occur in real life and it is sickening to think about. Some people cannot disconnect entertainment from reality and they are not wrong to invest so much into reality that they cannot enjoy violence in movies, they are just different from folks who do. I understand. But, also, *Sleepy Hollow* makes heads getting lopped off so much fun! The camera angles, the energy, the atmosphere, more, more, chop off all their heads! I love it!

Sleepy Hollow is a Tim Burton film based off the short story *The Legend of Sleepy Hollow*. The original story was published in the 1800s and was written by Washington Irving. The movie steers the headless horseman and all characters away from the original plot and has Ichabod Crane as a constable visiting the place known as Sleepy Hollow to investigate a series of murders. He has heard the tales of a supernatural killer but aims to prove that a human is actually behind the ghastly murders. It is an R-rated romp blending off-kilter humor and horror with a dash of romance. I bought a copy of this movie as a 4K collector's edition that I thought super neat because there is a copy of the Washington Irving story printed inside the steelbook case as a little book.

Johnny Depp stars as Ichabod Crane and Christina Ricci plays Katrina Van Tassel, a woman for whom Crane develops romantic feelings. I have read that Depp found the casting of Ricci a little weird for him because he had known her since she was a small child. That's creeper ole Hollywood for ya.

Crane is smitten and some lines between he and Katrina regarding that are what I always first recall about the film. They really tie the vibes of the movie together for me:

"…perhaps there is a little bit of witch in you, Katrina."

"Why do you say that?"

"Because you have bewitched me."

Those romantic lines are so corny and B movie appropriate and *Sleepy Hollow* leans into that for humor with the lead actor Depp maybe leaning too far, for sure farther than everyone else, but the other elements in play do not let the campy moments steal the show or ruin it.

Sleepy Hollow is a movie that I have returned to several times in life forgetting certain elements. I am not saying I get bored and tune out but every time I watch it I start to recall the convoluted plot behind why the horseman is lopping off heads and I start to think it is too much, but then by the end of the movie I am like: I like this movie. I've enjoyed it every time I've watched it.

Ichabod Crane is not the strongest hero, a bit timid and frightened, and I do not think even when he does rise to conducting actions of heroism he somehow doesn't really redeem himself for past, natural actions. Sure, he dares to battle the headless horseman, but he also uses a small child as a human shield when he is scared to go inside a spooky cave in the woods to confront a witch. Now, having said that, I do have to also say I find it entertaining when after he first sees the headless horseman he becomes a scaredy cat hiding in his room, clutching his sheets in fright. However, he uses that time to think and confront his fear and energies from his room with a peppy "let's go fight a ghost" energy that I found inspiring.

I just mentioned the spooky witch in the cave. She has a moment where her eyes pop out and her face goes all scary in such a manner that I am reminded of Large Marge from an earlier Tim Burton film, *Pee-Wee's Big Adventure*. The Large Marge moment terrified me as a kid—I am sure that the witch from this movie has had the same effect on a different generation.

Christopher Walken portrays the Headless Horseman in the movie which makes the killer a little less threatening when he has his head on his shoulders. Or maybe the fact that he is slightly silly looking makes him even scarier? The way his hair stands up makes Walken visually a fit for what Burton does though and reminds me of the fact that Walken also got a little funky with his villain hair for Burton in the 1992 movie *Batman Returns* as Max Shreck.

It is at around one hour and fifteen minutes into *Sleepy Hollow* that the investigating of Crane gets dull as a plot. Right as I want to say that aloud to the actors on the screen, a lot of action kicks off and the film is racing. The twisted plot about who is controlling the horseman and having him murder people is not something that makes me tune into the movie time and again over the years. The head lopping, the way pale Johnny Depp keeps getting blood spurting onto him, and the Horseman atop his steed hurdling out of a bleeding tree are all grand fun though.

There is a scene where a target of the Horseman runs into a church and the killer cannot follow after because the church is holy ground or something. The method he devises to spear his target and yank him out of a window into reach of his sword is a memorable moment of action to me. The horse galloping, sword swinging, and the grand explosion of a windmill all speak to my inner action movie fan. *Sleepy Hollow* just has a bit of everything.

Ichabod Crane might use children as human shields but Katrina during one scene actually steps in front of Crane as if to protect him and, though nothing in the movie is said to draw attention to this detail, I took notice. I think it is a sweet detail about what sort of person she is and maybe she can actually help Crane have some character arc down the road of their relationship in the happily ever after. Her stepping between him and danger in that moment reminded me of a scene from when I was a kid on the playground. It was pre-school and while I did not have any romantic intentions toward classmates my friend did have a girlfriend. One day during a game of tag, as the IT person cornered my friend, who was running alongside his girlfriend, I watched as she turned to face the IT and shielded her boyfriend from being tagged. Aww.

Visually my eyes actually had a hard time adjusting to the colors and lighting used in this movie. Perhaps it was due to this being my first intake of the 4K version, perhaps it was just my eyes were sore from staring at electronic screens all day. As the movie progressed, however, I grew accustomed to the way darkness and light were presented and there are some really cool color transitions in the film.

Sleepy Hollow is another movie with the unique touch of Tim Burton on full display. Fans of Tim Burton know what to expect in that artistic regard I think and in this case they are getting to see him play with material that one might not expect to have an R rating, but indeed, he took the classic tale into R territory with all the blood and head lopping. The movie won an Oscar for Best Art Direction-Set Direction with the golden statue being for the work done by Rick Heinrichs and Pete Young in bringing Burton's vision to life.

13. FRANKENSTEIN - 1931

The James Whale directed *Frankenstein* of 1931 was based off a 1927 play by Peggy Webling which was based off the 1818 novel by Mary Shelley. Therefore, in a creative adaptation sense it is no mystery how the film content got so far removed from the content of the classic book. This was my first time seeing the movie and it surprised me how many details from the book were retained in my memory, jiggled forth by seeing details in the film that "were not right." Yes, *Frankenstein* is another film where having read the book makes my favoritism lean toward the literature when it comes to how I want to remember the delivery of the story. I would have seen the monster visually from Halloween costumes and pop culture saturation and this film crafted that image. However, Mary Shelley's words fed into my imagination with the book and for me they were powerful enough to override classic Hollywood to put a monster upstairs in my attic that is a little different.

Frankenstein is called a "pre-code" movie and not being a film historian, I needed to look up that term. Pre-code Hollywood is the time period between 1927 and 1934 before the censorship guidelines of the Motion Picture Production Code, known as the Hays Code, began being enforced. They got away with a little more naughtiness in those early pictures. Of course, a lot of those naughty things weren't really all that naughty by the standards of today. I have read that *Frankenstein* was affected by some censorship anyway. The scene with the monster throwing the little girl into the lake was cut out and some dialog was snipped with Frankenstein exclaiming," Now I know what it feels like to be God!" Those elements were not returned into the film until the 1980s.

    An interesting dramatic film directed by Bill Condon, *Gods and Monsters*, explores the last days of Frankenstein director James Whale. It is speculative fiction based on the novel written by Christopher Bram. *Gods and Monsters* stars Ian McKellen as Whale with Brendan Fraser, a young man he develops a relationship of sorts with. The film won the 1999 Oscar for Best Writing, Screenplay Based on Material Previously Produced or Published. I recall what originally inspired me to watch the *Gods and Monsters* movie was not any knowledge about James Whale having been a monster movie director with a tragic end, suicide via pool drowning, but rather I was a fan of horror author Clive Barker and he served as an executive producer on the film—seeing his name had made me curious.

    The name Henry Frankenstein was the first detail to confuse me while watching *Frankenstein* because I always thought the man of science seeking to play God was Victor Frankenstein. Names have been swapped for the film; Henry is the scientist and he has a friend named Victor Moritz. Colin Clive portrays Henry and John Boles portrays Victor. Some other key characters and players are Mae Clarke as Elizabeth, Edward Van Sloan as Doctor Waldman, Frederick Kerr as Baron Frankenstein, and Dwight Frye as Fritz.

    In the opening Henry and his hunchback assistant

Fritz lurk about in a cemetery to watch a funeral. They hide and wait for the mourners to leave and the body to be buried. Then they sneak out and dig the body back up. I understand their need for body parts regarding sewing together their being to bring life into, but it did not make sense at all that they would stand there in the cemetery for so long watching the funeral and burial. They could have just sat at home and waited until late in the night or evening to return after the funeral.

    The acting in this movie is classic in style and not bad to experience; however, I found Fredrick Kerr as Baron Frankenstein to be inconsistent with the character. Maybe I am being too picky but his degrees of crankiness and just the way he carried the character differed from scene to scene in my opinion.

    Boris Karloff portrays the monster of the film and I think that in the early stages of life the monster and Karloff's performance are intriguing. His hand movements and confusion are well conveyed. As the film progresses I think he does fine but the schtick as it evolved with his yelling and violent actions was not as unsettling or interesting to me.

    The monster comes across a little girl portrayed by Marilyn Harris, Little Maria, and she wants him to play with her. She shows him how flowers float when she tosses them into the lake. He then grabs her and throws her into the lake. She does not surface. Off screen there was probably a cat laughing because prior to her being killed the little girl was holding that cat too tight. When in the hands of the girl the cat looked horrified in some shots. She is shown holding the cat when the monster arrives in one shot but then the cat magically disappears from her arms for the next shot and I have to think involving the cat at all was a mistake/poor production choice.

Violence toward the child was controversial for this film and got some of the footage edited. However, as I think about the cat being involved as the child's playmate I wonder if ever someone thought to have the monster kill the cat instead. Of course, this would take away the tragedy and need for revenge that the father fires up the town with, but they could have been driven by fear with the little girl tattling on the monster perchance. I have no idea why I am sitting here typing up a way that a movie in 1931 might have gotten around its censorship issues.

When the father of Maria brings her body into town and declares that she was murdered it does not make any sense. He was not there when the monster threw the girl into the lake. Why would he assume a monster threw his girl into the lake rather than she fell in and drowned?

The mad scientist activities and science fiction horror story elements are all in place within *Frankenstein* but the movie isn't really all that energized by those aspects. People talking and family drama elements eat up a good deal of time.

Henry makes his monster and after it kills Fritz, well, Henry realizes that there are consequences to playing God and he made a monster. He decides to go back to his life, home to marry his woman, and leave Doctor Waldman to clean up his mess ala euthanize the monster. The monster wakes up and kills the doctor to escape and go kill that girl. After that Henry, Victor, And

Elizabeth are at the Frankenstein home preparing for Henry to marry Elizabeth and the knowledge arrives that the monster has escaped. And then they hear some moaning that sounds like the monster. This sequence of events is very oddball. Henry seals his bride-to-be into her room for safety and runs off to locate the monster. He thinks it sounds as though it is upstairs, so upstairs they run. They search behind some junk and then hear noises again, this time deciding he must be in the cellar! Such goofy nonsense the searching with the punchline being that the monster sneaks through the bedroom window to attack Elizabeth.

Elizabeth survives her attack and the imagery of her splayed out on her bed afterward makes for some iconic horror imagery to me. Perhaps it is a screen still that I am just overly familiar with for some reason in my life of consuming visual media.

The final battle between the monster and his creator takes place inside a giant windmill. I know Tim Burton's *Sleepy Hollow* movie that I watched prior to this movie took inspiration from classic horror films and I have to think that this windmill might have been responsible for the giant windmill appearing and exploding in that film. During the fight there is a burning torch dropped on the ground and it looked to me like Colin Clive, or if he had a stunt double, fell onto it briefly. Ouch?

The monster throws Henry out of the windmill, an obvious dummy, no actor hurt there, and he hits one of the windmill blades, rides it a little, and then drops to the ground. It is hilarious looking to me and the fact that he survives is even funnier. The monster gets trapped in the windmill as the townsfolk set it on fire.

    Frankenstein the movie made me want to read the book again.

14. BARBARIAN - 2022

Barbarian was written and directed by Zach Cregger whom I am not familiar with in general but upon doing light research, one click, discovered he was involved with the sketch comedy group The Whitest Kids U'Know. I am familiar with a single sketch from this group having come across it several times on the Internet. It is a hilarious bit about men using hand gestures that signify "jerking off" as slang for "who cares" but one guy doesn't get it and takes things too far.

The trailer for the movie did a good job of leaving the premise as intrigue and I did not know what to expect going into it aside from a young woman arrives at a house that she has rented to discover that a man is already inside and claims to have also rented it. It's a big ole red herring flopping around for a bit before the crazy reality of what has been written storms out of some dark tunnels at the viewer. SPOILER ALERT!!!

Georgina Campbell plays Tess, who arrives at the rental to discover Keith inside, portrayed by Bill Skarsgård of Pennywise the Clown fame. The movie looks great and the actors are endearing. I think some of their early dialog discussing the dynamics of boy and girl relationships is very chunky and reminded me of some blocks of dialog I have written. However, I think the actors did a really good job of smoothing over the lines with their performances even if they did not sound 100% natural to my ear in the moment. Also, I have to say, the eyes of Georgina Campbell are wonderful.

This movie is full of social commentary involving toxic men and the woes of the world for women, and in the first section it is easy enough to sense that maybe Keith will turn out to be a creeper. Who knows, maybe he would be, but at the end of the first section of the movie his head gets bashed into bloody pulp against a wall by a tall, inbred monster woman.

Yes. The trailer had me thinking that some creepy perverts were probably inside the house waiting to take advantage of women. A room discovered by Tess with a camera tripod and mattress setup seemed to confirm such things. While this was true for the history of the house, the fact of the present in the story is that there is the "monster" living in tunnels below the house. The monster, called The Mother in the credits, captures Tess. Actor Matthew Patrick Davis is all dressed up to portray The Mother: think a female mutant from the *Wrong Turn* series as a nudist on steroids.

When Tess discovers the horror in the basement tunnels, the movie cuts away and introduces you to a new character named AJ. Justin Long portrays this character who is an actor in the middle of a crisis being fired from a television pilot due to his co-star going public with an accusation of rape. Long's performance is pitch-perfect in this movie. He is a horrible person that makes you laugh and it almost seems like he might get a chance to redeem himself for being a horrible person, but when faced with said chances he is always weak and doubles down on being a pathetic sort of evil.

AJ owns the house that Tess is captured under and he arrives there to prepare it for sale, needing the funds for his legal woes. It is hilarious to see his reaction to discovering the underground rooms in comparison to how Tess did. She was terrified and explored deeper into them only out of worry for the missing Keith. AJ sees the creepy spaces and is thrilled to have found extra square footage that he then goes to great lengths to measure out with a tape measure for his sale listing. It is while he is doing this that The Mother captures her second "baby."

It is here that the film goes back in time to a third section which shows the character Frank portrayed by Richard Brake. In the 80s he owned the house and was kidnapping and raping women in the underground spaces. The movie shows how he would stalk a woman and prepare her home for himself to enter sometime later. The things he actually got up to are explained later in the movie by a homeless man living on the street as he lets AJ and Tess know that the monster after them is the result of Frank breeding with captured women and them having babies and then him breeding with the babies making a copy of a copy until the inbred monstrous results of The Mother were created.

Frank is discovered still alive in the basement, elderly and in bed. It is kind of hard to fathom the timeline for such a monster having been born from his activities seeing him still alive. There are too many missing details if one stops to think too long about the history of the house really.

The fourth section of the movie returns to AJ and Tess in captivity. It is funny, gross, and unsettling to see The Mother trying to feed AJ with a dirty, giant bottle, stray hairs clinging to the moist nipple, and then when he refuses he gets to have her tit in his mouth. Tess and AJ both get chances to escape and take them.

AJ ends up discovering Frank in his bed with The Mother refusing to follow into the room because she seems frightened. Frank doesn't look too intimidating really and when AJ discovers VHS tapes of Frank's crimes and tells him he will be calling the cops, Frank blows his own brains out. It is in that scene that perhaps one might ponder how many degrees really separate Frank and AJ as men when it comes to taking advantage of women?

Tess goes through an ordeal to get the police to come to the house in order to rescue AJ. When the police are no help, she ends up in a battle with The Mother that results in her smashing the being into the house with her car. Tess could have escaped and been safe this whole time but she goes back to save AJ. When she goes down into the tunnels AJ shoots her with the gun he got off of Frank. You see this coming and it gets under your skin knowing it is about to happen. Thankfully Tess is not killed.

The Mother is not dead, Tess' vehicle does not work, and AJ has lost his keys. They run to hide near a water tower where a homeless man portrayed by Jaymes Butler resides. He says they are safe there and tells his guests the history of the house and monster. At this point AJ is feeling like a guilty monster and has a small monologue about thinking he is a bad person but he can fix things, determined not to let Tess die because he has shot her.

"I don't know if I'm a bad person. But I might be. I might be a bad person. Or maybe I'm a good person who just did a bad thing. I can't change what I've done. I can just try and fix it. And that's what I'm going to do. I'm going to fix it."

The Mother bursts into the area and kills the homeless man by ripping his arm off and beating him with it. AJ and Tess run for their lives—fenced in, they climb to the top of the water tower and become trapped. AJ fumbles and drops the gun. As The Mother comes up the stairs after them AJ proves to be true to who he really is and grabs the wounded Tess and shoves her off the water tower as bait to get The Mother to leave him alone.

"Hey! Come get your baby!"

The slow-motion shots of Tess plummeting to her doom and then The Mother diving off the tower after her go from emotional devastation for Tess to awesome goofiness seeing the monster diving. It is this moment that serves as a hinge for the movie experience and left me to wonder whether or not I was swinging my thoughts toward it ruins the entire thing or is acceptable. Tess fell first and then after a bit the monster dives after her but somehow the monster ends up under Tess saving he from the fall. It bugged me after first watching the movie that the laws of gravity were ignored.

I enjoyed the craziness of the movie so much though that gravity ultimately does not matter. Maybe The Mother, a being of crazy existence to begin with, can indeed defy the laws of gravity. I have heard of mothers lifting cars off of trapped children—why couldn't a mutant fly down and save their perceived child?

AJ discovers Tess is still alive and goes right back to his acting out remorse. He does not have too long to wallow in having to exist as himself because The Mother is still alive as well. She pops up, grabs AJ, and smooshes his eyes out while crushing his head.

The gun is on the street near where Tess lies. The Mother turns to Tess and can see that she is hurt. The Mother is sad for her baby and wants to take her home. It is an amazing setup how the monster is truly caring for her baby and once again Georgina Campbell has amazing acting eyes. Tess lifts the gun up and puts it point blank against the face of The Mother. The Mother kisses its creepy fingers and touches them to the head of her baby. Tess pulls the trigger—blam, cue the credits and the song *Be My Baby* by The Ronettes.

I really loved that final shot with the transition to the credits and song. During the credits Tess is shown to get to her feet and walk her wounded self down it, a survivor with a new lease on life.

I have no clue why the movie is titled *Barbarian*. It sounds like the writer of the film doesn't have a solid answer beyond he wrote it as a place holder and then just chose to keep it as that. It does leave room for one to try and think and interpret for themselves a reason for the piece to be titled *Barbarian* I suppose. The street they were on was something like Barbary Street so maybe the residents of it are Barbarians. Or, of course, one can think about how brutish men can be: Frank, AJ, maybe even Keith, how there is a potential barbarian in them all.

Barbarian was a nice treat. I think the line it toes of being too obvious in its social commentary is blurred by the craziness of The Mother. As someone who has criticized some of Jordan Peele's work as being too "on the nose" regarding social commentary I am fully aware of me now clapping my hands and being like, "who cares, bring out the freak!" Now, who wants warm milk?

15. PSYCHO - 1960

Alfred Hitchcock is considered filmmaking royalty. His movie *Psycho* is Horror Hall of Fame material, a classic that has inspired not only fear in viewers but other films wishing to capture the applauded magic. And I have never actually bothered to watch it until now.

Everyone knows *Psycho* whether they have seen it or not. The shower scene is iconic and copycat scenes are a dime a dozen. There are lines in the movie that transcend the genre and are known by mainstream Hollywood fans worldwide. The most popular being: "I'll lick the stamps." Okay, maybe not that line. I liked it though. It is said as a part of a romantic fantasy between people wishing to escape and I felt the power behind them. These are the popular quotations: "A boy's best friend is his mother," and "We all go a little mad sometimes." Yeah, I guess that last one is just as powerful as "I'll lick the stamps."

Psycho stars Janet Leigh as Marion Crane who steals $40,000 from her job and drive offs to start a new life somewhere. However, when she stops for the night at a struggling motel she meets Norman Bates and hears his grumpy mother. Anthony Perkins stars as Norman Bates and if you want to save yourself the trouble of sitting through the feature he is a psycho who also thinks he is his dead mother. He kills people as his dead mother. The movie is based on a 1959 novel written by Robert Bloch.

Janet Leigh as Marion carries the first part of the

film, intriguing as the woman on the run. She is utilized as sex appeal but also, even being morally compromised as a thief, she is someone who can easily be identified with and makes for a solid lead. Of course, she is the victim in the epic shower scene. Norman shows up with a knife and stabs the woman to death as the soundtrack screeches out those iconic notes that even as someone who had never watched the movie knew by heart. It seems pretty obvious that movies such as *Friday the 13th* took soundtrack notes when they were taking Horror Movie Making 101 and learning from the successes of the past.

When the leading character is killed audiences are then given the support characters to follow as they try to find out what happened to Marion. These roles are filled by the likes of John Gavin as Sam Loomis, Vera Miles as Lila Crane, and Martin Balsam as Milton Arbogast. There are many more but these are the key players having experiences at the Bates Motel and coming into contact with Norman Bates in the wild.

Before her brutal death, Marion hits the road and drives with severe paranoia being her passenger. A police officer checks on her when she is taking a roadside nap and then follows her to the next town. As she tries to sell her car, trade it in for new wheels to keep the law off her trail, Marion can see that the cop who chatted with her roadside sits across the street watching her. If she was trying to throw the law off her trail and going to the trouble to change cars, it really doesn't make any sense that she would go ahead with the vehicle deal. The cop watching her has seen her new wheels which defeats the entire purpose of her being at the dealership.

The shower scene lives up to its hype as a piece of movie making history. Janet Leigh's presence was strong during all her screen time but when she is dead it makes for the most powerful image in the entire film. Sure, the tearing away of the shower curtain, the knife, and the shrieking are memorable; however, the most important part of the entire movie to me, the most haunting image is when Marion keels over the side of the tub and her dead face rests against the floor. The camera work and the way it lingers on her face makes the loss of her life devastating.

The rest of the movie is painfully boring. *Psycho* is an overrated snoozer.

The boredom got heavy right after Marion is killed. Norman works to clean up the crime scene and dispose of the body. The camera stays with Norman and lets the audience watch this dull process. It is creepy for the average person to see the steps a psycho will go through to hide his crime, but the tension is a product of its time and probably played more intensely in 1960 than it did to me in 2023.

The second murder comes with some quirky camera work showing Milton the detective being stabbed and then falling down some stairs. It is memorable on a visual level but not as compelling and tragic as Marion's death. After that the investigation and all the people standing around talking as they try to figure out what happened to Marion: boring, boring.

Eventually Lila Crane, sister to Marion, and Sam, lover to Marion, arrive at the Bates motel and uncover Norman's secret. Lila finds the corpse of his mother and as Norman comes up behind her with a knife Sam grabs Norman from behind. It is a very weak end scenario and as Sam grabs Norman the killer pulls some faces that would make Jim Carey proud and just kind of melts weirdly into Sam's arms. I do not understand why he gave up so easily and think there should have been more of a struggle. I get that Norman is his mother in that moment and weak in general but Sam just grabbing him to defeat him was lame.

Once Norman is captured the movie is not over. There is a long section at the police station where a psychiatrist tries to explain Norman's condition and it is not interesting at all. Another product of its time I suppose, shocking in 1960, but not so much now.

Psycho is a boring movie and I found myself daydreaming about what I would do to make a better ripoff of the feature to throw onto the pile of knockoffs that already exist.

16. IT - 2017

The 1986 Stephen King novel *It* is one that I have read but it did not stick with me; wouldn't be able to tell you any details from it though I do recall details from many of his other books that I read at around the same window of age. The 1990 mini-series movie *It* starring Tim Curry affected a lot of people with coulrophobia but like the novel I did not become a fan. The 2017 reboot of *It* as a film is slick as a production and I have found it to be the more compelling version of the material.

It Chapter One was directed by Andy Muschietti who was born in Argentina and made a splash into the horror genre by getting his 2008 Spanish language short film *Mama* expanded into an English feature film in 2013 starring Jessica Chastain. A trio of writers hold the screenplay credit for Muschietti's take on the Stephen King material: Chase Palmer, Cary Joji Fukunaga, and Gary Dauberman.

The story for this film follows a group of kids who deal with different dramas and traumas in their lives at the same time that they have to face off against an entity of evil that takes on the form of a clown called Pennywise. As a coming-of-age film I think this section of the story is more compelling than *It Chapter 2* that follows the characters as adults. In fact, I can do a mini-review of the continuation film with the adults and say that I recall being bored and not caring about the characters anymore. It seemed like they had a lot on the line emotionally as kids but then as adults transformed into caricatures.

    The cast of kids is an ensemble with Bill portrayed by Jaeden Martell seeming like the main character though *Stranger Things* fans probably recognize Finn Wolfhard as Richie in the supporting role first and foremost. Jeremy Ray Taylor as Ben, Chosen Jacobs as Mike, Jack Dylan Grazer as Eddie, Wyatt Oleff as Stanley all get ample screen time as well. Young Sophia Willis is really the lone female amongst the boys as Beverly and when it comes to acting I think she puts in the strongest performance. She was not in *Stranger Things* but she did have her own teenage Netflix show *I Am Not Okay with This* that I thought was entertaining but it was disappointing that it did not get a second season.

    The movie opens up with a scenario that sets the tone and lets you know you are in for an R-rated experience that is not going to spare the kiddos from any violence. Georgie portrayed by Jackson Robert Scott meets Pennywise as the clown is hanging out, peeking out of a sewer drain and the clown rips the child's arm off. Yikes! I am not one that is normally applauding horror movies that hurt very small children but I think that the savagery was important for making It work because it really kept Pennywise and his odd voice and movements from being 100% creepy not silly. Bill Skarsgard puts in a very creative performance as Pennywise.

    A movie such as *It* sounds like a nightmare to have to direct to me because of it having such a large cast of children. Directing actors can be a demanding babysitting job with adults, so, teens and younger can double down on the stress, their attention spans often short, if trying to get moving performances out of them. The results are a mixed bag but the acting never ruined the movie or threw me out of the experience.

What did almost throw me out of the experience? The heavy usage of CGI. Sometimes the herky jerky clown antics would be too goofy. Yet, when I think on it, I also can see how the CGI usage amplifies the overall weirdness of Pennywise and might make him all the more unsettling for some folks.

Certain story elements are amped up maybe too much as well. Some attempts at comedy go lame, the banter between Eddie and Richie doesn't always land but then again, kids CAN be really talkative and annoying I suppose. The main bully in the film, Henry portrayed by Nicholas Hamilton, goes a bit too far. I do not recall the details from the book, I'd wager the bullies in the book are just as intense as the film, but the fact that Henry is able to get away with carving letters into the flesh of another kid without consequences seems like a stretch.

There is heavy sex appeal thrust on to the character Beverly with the men around her all being lusty maniacs it seems. Her own father appears to be a molester, there is an interaction with a leering pharmacist, and then of course the young boys have a crush on her. Eventually there is a scene where the boys gaze upon her as she sunbathes in her underwear and if the way this scene was shot makes some people uncomfortable I understand that, considering all of the perv crap that has happened to child actors in Tinseltown. There is the thought that having a group of young boys and one girl hanging out in their underwear for an extended amount of time in a movie is creepy, it could have been shot in a different manner or different scenes portraying the same elements that were desired for the character interactions to have been devised. Or one can think about how it is trying to play true to a time period or the reality of that is how the kids would have gone swimming.

My favorite scene in the movie is when Beverly is in her bathroom and the hair in the sink drain shoots out to snatch her. Then gallons of blood gush forth drenching her and the room. A room getting coated in blood might not be the most original horror visual but sometimes it just works.

In the climax of the movie Finn Wolfhard gets the best line delivery moment for the film facing off against Pennywise. Yes all of the talk about floating is very quotable but I always first think about the end battle when some of the kids get the choice to escape, yet remain to help Bill, who is in the clutches of Pennywise. It is Richie who talks in a manner that seems like maybe he will flee, listing all the reasons he should, but instead sticks it out: "I told you, Bill. I fucking told you. I don't want to die. It's your fault. You punched me in the face. You made me walk through shitty water. You brought me to a fucking crackhead house. And now…I'm gonna have to kill this fucking clown."

It is not perfect but it surprised me and I found there to be some strong moments and some entertaining moments.

17. BONES AND ALL - 2022

Going into my viewing of *Bones and All* I knew it had something to do with cannibals or monsters but it would have been really cool to have turned the movie on at random without the prior glimpses given via the trailer. Ah, romance and eating people go together like peanut butter and Jeffrey Dahmner. I am reminded of a terrible song I wrote when I was a child with the lyrics, "eat the ones you love, it becomes you as it flows inside, eat the ones you love but don't choke on the mistakes." Of course, that has nothing to do with nothing and the movie *Bones and All* is something; I tell you what.

Luca Guadagnino directed *Bones and All* and he is no stranger to the horror genre with 2018 remake of *Suspiria* also being his handiwork. The screenplay was written by David Kajganich who wrote on Guadagnino's films *A Bigger Splash* and *Suspiria*. The source material that the screenplay was based on is the 2015 novel by Camille DeAngelis. The book won a 2016 Alex Award which honors stories written for adults with special appeal to young adults ages 12-18. The special story here is that a young woman who is an "eater" is left behind by her father after she bites off another girl's finger at a sleepover. The man cannot cover for his daughter's "needs" any longer and she sets off across the country on her own to find her mother. In route she discovers other cannibals such as herself and develops a close relationship with a young man; aww, they fall in love.

Taylor Russell stars as the leading lady Maren and I recognized her from having watched the Netflix rendition of *Lost in Space*, a show where she portrayed Judy Robinson. Her romantic interest and partner in crime is Lee portrayed by Timothee Chalamet who worked with the director previously on the film *Call Me by Your Name*. Mark Rylance is Sully in the film, a troubled cannibal who gives in to his most creepy whims while trying to combat years of loneliness. Michael Stuhlbarg, whom I always remember firstly from *Boardwalk Empire* as Arnold Rothstein, makes a memorable though brief appearance in the film as does David Gordon Green who most would know as a movie director not an actor, ala Green directed the *Halloween* horror trilogy of films released 2018, 2021, and 2022. Chloe Sevigny is Janelle.

The acting in this film does have some spotty moments where I felt the actors were reciting memorized lines more than naturally feeling the material and making it "real." However, this did not become distracting for any length of time. I think the way Taylor Russell spoke as her character when dealing with Sully was actually quite good.

In one scene Taylor Russell is in tears and a snotty booger gloops out of her nose. The actress proceeds to wipe at her nose and manages to smear the booger onto her cheek for a moment before wiping it away. I cannot say that I see that too often in films; give her an award!

Mark Rylance does a stellar job with the character Sully. He is an older cannibal who gives Maren some solid advice and even feeds her a meal. I found myself thinking him a little "off' but harmless. However, as the movie progresses and he keeps popping up one realizes that his nice intentions have been stirred too deep by loneliness and the man is a stalker with a lit fuse, a bomb close to going off.

The opening scenes of the movie felt like a horror film from the 1980s or early 1990s. It was a vibe that drew me right in and then when she bites that girl's finger the shock value is still strong even if I saw it coming from the movie trailer.

As I was watching the cannibal humans feed in this film I wondered what gave them the ability to gnaw through human flesh so easily. I did not see fangs or anything like that. The origins of why they are cannibals is never explained but that adds to the angst within the story, young people, err, young monsters trying to find their place in a world that they do not fit into, not knowing why they are the way that they are.

Maren tracks down her mother, Janell, finds her locked away in an asylum having eaten her own arms off. This discovery that her mother passed along the eating condition to her seems like it could be helpful for the young woman's journey but then her mother attacks her! Her mother knows that she has created a monster and has been waiting for the child to one day find her so that she might kill her. The moment when she lunges at her is just as strong a shock sort of scare as when Maren bites the finger off the teen earlier in the movie.

The classic come together then break apart romance play is in effect for this story and Maren struggling with her condition and not wishing to kill people for food leaves Lee for a spell. They get back together after she has some time to herself and they set about figuring out how to lead normal lives. This is when Sully returns and attacks them. I am a sucker for tragic romance stories and *Bones and All* gave me a strong dose of the sad good stuff.

It is a gory end fight with Sully and Lee becomes mortally wounded. He does not wish for Maren to get him help because he fears the bloody scene of their apartment will lead to too many questions. He coaxes her into eating him. I imagine she ate him bones and all. There's that goofy old lyric of mine popping into my head again, "eat the ones you love."

Did Lee need to die? It occurred to me that they still could have called for help and explained the bloody mess as them having just fended off a psycho. However, I guess during the fight Karen did pull out some of Sully's organs, so, maybe that fact added to their paranoia about cops having too many questions and Lee's dramatic decision that he should die for Maren to remain free from scrutiny.

The music for the film was handled by Trent Reznor and Atticus Ross. In the end scene as Lee is dying, Trent Reznor's voice arrives in song and I have to admit the editing in that moment was timed a little too close to some mouth movements by Lee and for a second I thought he was singing and the movie was going full blown musical. The song is *You Made it Feel Like Home* and works perfectly regarding enhancing the emotional turmoil of the end events.

Bones and All does not follow Maren beyond this horrible turn of events with Lee and Sully. The viewer is left to wonder what becomes of her and how she moves on with her unusual life. I find my curiosity about the character's future to be a good thing and do not mind it being unknown—this helps my own imagination do some emotional stretching and thought exercises.

Bones and All is my type of movie, good stuff.

18. THE WOLFMAN - 2010

The Wolfman of 2010 is a remake of the 1941 Universal monster movie *The Wolf Man*. I have never seen the classic film but did watch this one when it was released in theaters and it did not leave a sticking impression.

Joe Johnston directed *The Wolfman* and prior to this film he helmed features such as *Honey, I Shrunk the Kids, The Rocketeer, Jumanji, and Jurassic Park III*. I can recall being a huge fan of 1989's *Honey, I Shrunk the Kids* as a kid myself but none of Johnston's other early work really clicked with me. Prior to directing, Joe Johnston worked on visual effects for some big George Lucas projects ala the original *Star Wars* trilogy and *Raiders of the Lost Ark*. The year after *The Wolfman* he was the director for *Captain America: The First Avenger*.

It sounds like Joe Johnston got the gig for directing this film because they wanted to strike a balance for a broad target audience. Aside from the fans of the classic, they need to sell merchandise to younger folks more accustomed to the action-packed werewolf antics of say the *Underworld* film series. The action sequences are what kept me interested in the film and I would say that the right director was at the wheel for that reason alone. When the wolf attacked I thought that the bang was there for the buck for sure.

Visually the film is interesting as the loud attack sequences of the wolf are paired with 1800s settings that at times made me think: what if Tim Burton had directed this? Helping the Burton vibe is the fact that his frequent musical collaborator Danny Elfman scored the film. However, even though the bulk of the music came from Elfman it is said that his original score was altered by others, including newly composed sections, as the film changed over the course of production and his original pieces did not altogether fit the finished vision.

    Aside from finding myself drawn into the bloody wolf action I think this film succeeds in paying homage to the original film with the look of the world. Even though I grew up on different werewolf films I am familiar with the way Lon Chaney Jr. got made up to look wolfy in the original. Rick Baker took that original look and injected some steroids into it but the end result was very cool looking in my opinion with the design of the facial features being where the classic inspiration growls through; there is more man allowed to show through the beast I think. Rick Baker won the 2011 Oscar for Best Achievement in Makeup for *The Wolfman*. Prior to the 2011 Oscar he also won Academy Awards for his work on *An American Werewolf in London*, *Harry and the Hendersons*, *Ed Wood*, *The Nutty Professor*, *Men in Black*, and *How the Grinch Stole Christmas*.

    The story for the film centers around Larence Talbot returning home to help find a missing brother. He meets up with his father and the woman that aimed to marry his brother only to discover that his sibling has already been found dead, a presumed victim of some wild beast. The suspicious townsfolk think that a performing bear at a nearby gypsy camp is to blame for the attacks but they soon realize they are facing off against something crazier in the form of a werewolf. During an attack Talbot is bitten by the wolf and upon surviving finds himself cursed to transform into a bloodthirsty beast when the moon is full. Becoming a werewolf doesn't stop him from trying to avenge his brother, as well as his mother, and when he finds out that his father is the werewolf, well, family politics get beastly. Andrew Kevin Walker and David Self share the screenplay credit for the film with Curt Siodmak also getting a credit for the original 1941 script that served as inspiration.

    Benicio Del Toro stars as Lawrence Talbot and is said to have been pursuing the role forever due to being a huge fan of the classic film. Del Toro is an interesting actor and his quirks have made many other films magical. I could not make up my mind on whether or not he was throwing off my ability to really get into *The Wolfman* or not. Sometimes she would deliver lines in a manner that in ever so subtle a way felt to me like they did not fit with the atmosphere around him. It felt like "acting," with his performance tricks too obvious. However, I cannot say that his performance alone was what makes me lean toward saying the action sequences are the saving grace of the film because I think the overall framework of the story and the way the plot unfurled is what really made things shaky.

    Emily Blunt stars as Gwen Conliffe, the bride to be left in mourning, only she never really gets to go in too distraught of a direction because apparently she and Lawrence are going to have a romantic connection. The romance between Gwen and Lawrence is a major key to the entire plot but it doesn't fit the creative lock exactly in my opinion. I did not buy the chemistry between the characters and Gwen's passion for Lawrence by the end all felt too forced, their love more nonsensical than a man changing into a wolf at the full moon. Love is weird though in general I suppose. Blunt's screen presence is strong in the film overall though and I think she helped the settings running around in her time period dresses. Personally, I did not recall her being in the movie even though I was aware of her as an actress at that time with her having starred in the 2008 released film *Sunshine Cleaning* which I like a lot.

      Anthony Hopkins is Sir John Talbot and I think his acting performance was the best. He out-quirks Benicio Del Toro in some line deliveries but I think he landed them with some fun. Later in the film I think his lines and actions taken get rather silly but that Hopkins rolled along well regarding his work as an actor.

      Hugo Weaving is another main character in the form of Aberline, the lawman who comes to track down the killer. He does a fine job but more or less I think any actor could have stepped into the shoes of the character with his storyline being rather dull. At the end of the film Aberline has been wounded and would be the next in line to become a wolf I suppose. I would not be opposed to watching Hugo Weaving struggle with transforming into a murderous beast in a film.

      The Talbot family have a servant who is also on the grounds of their rich family estate and that is Singh portrayed by Art Malik. This character seems like someone who can handle himself and has been juggling the family werewolf secret for a long time. I thought he would play a more important part in the later action of the film but he is killed off screen and his body just discovered hanging around.

There isn't really much of a "mystery" aspect to the film. I think the reveal of John Talbot being the troublesome werewolf is somewhat predictable but some may not see it coming. However, I think what ruined the intrigue aspect of things for me was that after Lawrence is bitten it is well-known that he will become a werewolf. I know, you as a viewer go into the film knowing that, but inside the movie world the gypsies who save his life after he is mauled know what he will become, and in their discussions over the morality of saving him even though he will become a killer, well, any intrigue was sapped for me. Why did they save him? Their prior knowledge of werewolves did not stand alone as a factor that did not gel well for me but paired with the way the townsfolk are portrayed, I do not know, the story math was off. The townsfolk are somewhat being treated like religious zealots frightened by silly legends of monsters. However, THEY ARE RIGHT! THERE IS A KILLER BEAST! They are the warrior heroes of the tale!

The dramatic conflict of son vs father is interesting enough. However, the dialog bringing all of it to life was never impactful for me. One moment that stood out, though not between father and son, were some lines that felt like they were meant to end the scene with strong "oh my gosh" energy. Lawrence sees the ammo that Singh keeps around and they have this exchange:

"Silver? I didn't know you hunted monsters."

"Sometimes monsters hunt you."

The men stare at each other, the lines hang heavy in the air, the scene ends, and I thought: what nonsense was that? Those lines seemed like they were meant to carry some real impact but to me they were meaningless gibberish.

The final showdown between father and son in wolf form is fun regarding visuals and action but lame in conclusion. Daddy wolf bites his son and throws him around the room, obviously the stronger combatant, as the room catches on fire around them. However, Lawrence ends up winning the fight with a late kick upward of his legs that sends mean old dad into the fireplace to burn. He does jump out aflame and Lawrence finishes the job by smacking his head off but for some reason I thought the moment with the kick and wolfman daddy sailing through the air was goofy. I am nit-picking though and it was an accumulation of different production elements not stirring up well enough within my brain that led to my disappointment in this moment probably.

The opening of their battle perhaps set the tone off on the wrong foot for me and made me more critical of it all. Lawrence has some silver shotgun shells loaded into what I thought was a shotgun and when he goes to shoot John the gun does not fire. John states: "I removed the powder from those shells years ago." Why would he have removed the powder from the shells years ago? As a prank for this exact moment? Why wouldn't he have just thrown them away instead? Obviously to take away Singh's ability to shoot him while letting the man think he still held the power is what I deduced but then I thought: shotgun shells don't even work like that. If he took the powder out of the shells that does not stop the gun itself from firing it just means the shells would have banged off without spraying out any contents, right? And wait, they looked like bullets not shells. Shotguns use shells, rifles use bullets, maybe I am confused, maybe someone got their weaponry and ammunitions crossed. I thought Singh showed off bullets but the latter ammo and weapon is a shotgun.

The ending of the film disappointed me as well. Gwen finds that her love for Lawrence is not powerful enough to get through the beast in him quick enough and she has to shoot him dead. This sounds like a tragic scenario that I would normally eat up but I did not buy into their love and her quest to save him felt like time-filler for the feature more than not. The open ending with Aberline having been bitten just adds more disappointment as a punctuation mark for me.

The Wolfman manages to have some bloody rampages in it that are entertaining and the cast do a mixed job of mixing with said action to make the film watchable. However, the story and the drama needed to hook me did not work, something was amiss, and I cannot say *The Wolfman* was all that great.

19. MALEVOLENT - 2018

Malevolent is an adjective meaning "having or showing a wish to do evil to others."

The 2018 film *Malevolent* opens with a cool quote: "None of the dead come back. But some stay." - St. John the Divine.

Olaf de Fleur Johannsesson directed *Malevolent* and while that is a fun name to try and pronounce, typing it over and over would be a chore. I do not recognize any of the other films he has directed prior to this Netflix released film that is considered a British production. Olaf was born in Iceland.

The screenplay was written by Ben Ketai and Eva Konstantopoulos with the novel *Hush* by Konstantopoulos being the source material that it was based upon. Eva appears to have a bunch of children's television writing credits, while the works that I recognize from Ketai's writing credits are the genre films *The Forest* and *The Strangers: Prey at Night*.

The story of the film involves a group of ghosthunters that are frauds but then on their latest case they encounter real ghosts.

To be critical: anyone could have written or directed *Malevolent*. It is a very dull by the numbers affair without any dramatic flair or visuals in any department. Well, okay, the sound design was good with the attempts to put some jolt into scares for the film, though "scares" are lacking overall. Aside from that, the pacing and the plot limp along like the character Elliot, portrayed by Scott Chambers in the film, after he hurts his leg.

Florence Pugh stars as Angela and I like her voice when she is pretending to be coming back into consciousness. As talented as Pugh is, she alone does not make this movie interesting in the least bit. She also seemed super short in this movie. The Internet says she is about five foot two.

The second member of the cast who does a solid job regarding presence is Celia Imrie as Mrs. Green. The second she arrives, however, you know that something is amiss and that the twist is that either she is a killer or her killer son is still on the haunted grounds.

Ben Llyod-Hughes, Scott Chambers, and Georgina Bevan are the main leads aside from Florence Pugh but none of them really stood out. Bevan really does not have much to do in the film at all aside from being a body to rack up the death count. Ben Lloyd-Hughes does a solid enough job of making the character Jackson unlikable though I suppose even if I didn't really get enough energy from any of the performances to want to write to you about them with kudos.

There is a scene in which Angela visits her grandpa. He catches her looking at a photograph of her mother who had mental issues and is dead; clawed her own eyes out. Grandpa says something along the lines of "I guess we will talk about what we always talk about." That was not an exact quote but he alludes to she always wants to talk about her mother. A little later in the scene she looks at a photo of her mother and asks her grandpa "What was she like?" This generic question seemed odd to me considering it was already established that they have previously talked in great length about her mother.

Old video footage can be spooky and *Malevolent* features a lot of shots that are from the movie camera that the character Elliot carries around to film the events. It never got very spooky to me though and it failed to bring any production value to the proceedings in my opinion. In fact, their camera becomes a problematic prop to me when it is shown that they leave it running during scenes where they talk about things they would not want their viewer to hear because they are doing a con. Are the characters that dumb?

When the characters and pieces of the story start moving around in the end scenario the storytellers show off their inability to move puzzle pieces around in a manner that is compelling or even logical. There is a car crash and the killer drags one guy away to let ole mommy torture but leaves the other two lying there? The old lady and her son state they have to kill the ghosthunters just like they did the little girls in the past so that no one will come snooping around the grounds again. So, why did she even invite them there in the first place? I suppose she really was hearing the ghost children and thought the ghosthunters might help her and then turns on them after she realizes they are frauds, but still it all felt goofy. The old lady is sewing people's mouths shut and whacking a spike into their heads with a hammer while they are tied to a chair—such an elaborate little ritual of nonsense.

Angela gets tied to a chair, after being magically put to sleep, via choking, for the amount of time it would take to drag her there and tie her up. She calls upon the ghost girls from the past, who are not scary looking in the least, and gets them to scream. This scream distracts the killer old lady so much that Angela can get free and arm herself to kill the lady. Prior to that the killer son was dispatched by Elliot who comes into the room and stabs him. Does that sound like action? It is poorly staged and lifeless.

Pugh's character gets to survive and the movie ends on an ominous note with a shadow crossing over her as she looks up and tells her grandpa on the phone, "I'm not alone." It seems to imply that she can see ghosts but you already know she can if you watched the rest of the movie; therefore, I do not really know what impact that scene was supposed to have as the final goodbye of this claptrap.

Malevolent brings nothing fresh feeling to this type of genre piece: ghosts want you to know who really killed them. If you have seen one then you have seen this one and you have probably seen far better ones. The only reason to watch this is if you must watch all things Florence Pugh.

20. IT'S ALIVE - 1974

Born in 1974 the horror film *It's Alive* was somewhat abandoned right away regarding Warner Brothers promoting it. However, in 1977 someone decided that it was a project that they could put fresh energy into promoting and a creepy advertising campaign featuring a baby stroller helped the movie find its audience. I can recall seeing the ads for the film when I was a child, the baby stroller with the words "There's only one thing wrong with the Davis baby...*It's Alive*"

Larry Cohen wrote and directed this movie along with two sequels. By the time he died in 2019 at the age of 82 his directing credits numbered 21. His writing credits, however, stretch out to 88 projects across television and film with the *Maniac Cop* series being another genre property he penned. He did not just net B horror movie writing credits though. The 2002 thriller *Phone Booth* starring Colin Farrell was written by Larry Cohen and he also worked on the 2005 thriller *Cellular* starring Kim Basinger.

Frank and Lenore go to the hospital so that Lenore can give birth to their second child. The kid comes out of the womb as a murderous mutant, kills the entire team who helped it into the world, and then burrows on out of the ceiling of the hospital. Lt. Perkins is one of the officers tasked with hunting down the mutant as it crawls around the city killing more people. John P. Ryan stars as Frank with Sharon Farrell portraying his wife, while James

Dixon is Perkins.

There are some gags that were cute but I never felt like I was in a totally bent comedy movie. It all becomes more of a parental concern drama that I felt could have embraced the craziness of a mutant baby in an even more over-the-top fashion. *It's Alive* could have gone full *Basket Case* and been far more entertaining.

The film also serves as a reminder of the unsafe practices of the pharmaceutical industry as it is alluded to that killer mutant babies are being born thanks to the drugs pregnant women are taking.

There is an early gag that amused me. A group of men are in the hospital waiting room and one of them has the vending machine steal his change. Frank gives the man fifty cents to stop banging on the machine. Then you watch the guy go to a gumball machine and it appears that it too eats his money.

The best line in the movie is delivered by James Dixon. As Lt. Perkins stands over the corpse of one of the baby's victims he states: "Hunting and killing babies doesn't seem to be my specialty."

There is a scene where a milkman is killed in his truck. Bottles of milk spill out of the truck as he is being mauled and as they break and the milk flows in the street the baby cries. The camera stays on this milk spilling for a while and I wonder if they were trying to drive home a "crying over spilt" milk joke.

The ending showdown confused me a little bit. Frank has a change of heart and wants to protect his child while the police surround him ready to execute it. Instead of following the commands of the officers he throws the baby at one of them which I assume leads to that guy's demise because the guns start blazing to kill the baby. It seems like Frank should have been held accountable for doing that but instead he is given a pat on the back as he and his wife sadly prepare to leave the scene.

A killer baby movie needs more killer babies and less talking heads is my opinion. *It's Alive* is a short movie overall but I would like to have had more horror scenes. The glimpses that you get of the mutant baby are fun and Oscar winning Special Effects guru Rick Baker designed it.

This movie reminded me of a poem I wrote when I was kid. It is published in my book *Crap Poetry* but you don't have to buy that book to read it—here, have a copy of *Stupid Undead Baby Poem*:

> The flesh split apart like a pair of rosy lips
> The toothless hole drooled blood of incredible red
> The newborn would find a place amongst the crypts
> Life was delayed for the baby born dead
> Mother's screams were all in vain
> The eyes were sealed with crust
> Torn guts awarded for all her pain
> All rational thoughts gone bust
> Miserable and lonely, she howled into her death
> The snapping point came with the child she didn't save
> The life should have cried; bringing joy, inhaling breath
> Instead it found its way misplaced into a grave
>
> Time caught up in a couple of years
> Something stirred within the dirt

The infant blinked away some tears
Underground and born to hurt
The corpse it glowed with new-found soul
An amazing prize for one to find
The universe had lost control
Age was placed into its mind
Little hands dug out of the soil
Power given abnormally great
Voices fueled the intense turmoil
Whispering thoughts of murdering hate
Cloaked in shades of green-black rot
The creature crawled across the stones
Dead in body but in brain not
Terror squealed through moldy bones
New world so different from the womb
Driven by anger, fear, and shock
The infant risen from a tomb
Pushed aside rusty gate and lock

The creature roamed for several miles
Decaying along sidewalks and streets
Losing substance in ooky piles
Ready to sample the human meats
The baby attacked a passerby
Sharp grown teeth seeking blood
A monster child meant to die
Wearing a mask of burial mud
The passerby stomped its head
Killed the child's hold
Rendered the undead back to dead
No evil did unfold
What a stupid baby.

21. THE WRAITH - 1986

The 1986 film *The Wraith* is a flick that I found as a kid and it clicked with me. Perhaps this revenge tale helped inspire my love for the beyond the grave antics of *The Crow* released in 1994. The idea of tragedy not being the end of a story when it results in death is fascinating and darkly romantic to me. In *The Wraith* a gang of road racers find themselves being killed off by a mysterious force driving a crazy car. I can see how the blending of action and supernatural horror would have easily intrigued little kid me; adult me went into this fresh viewing intrigued as to whether or not the film could still set off any power vibrations through the emotional system within that is connected to art in the form of moving picture shows.

Mike Marvin wrote and directed *The Wraith*. I cannot say that I am familiar with any of his other directing or writing credits aside from recognizing some television shows he worked on episodes of: *MacGyver*, *Renegade*, and *Silk Stockings*.

I connected *The Wraith* to *The Crow* in my opening bit of this writing and the pictures can also be linked via the morbid trivia that people died while filming them. While a chase sequence was being filmed for *The Wraith* a camera car overturned and assistant cameraman Bruce Ingram was killed.

Both *The Crow* and *The Wraith* also feature characters named Skank who have possibly tortured their last remaining brain cells with chemicals. David Sherrill is the Skank of *The Wraith*; he enjoys drinking hydraulic fluid and huffing WD-40. The character named Skank in *The Crow* is portrayed by Angel David.

Charlie Sheen is the "movie star" lead of the movie though more time is spent with the villains than him. I have read that his part was shot in a very quick amount of time in what he called a "pit stop" on his way to go shoot the Oliver Stone film *Platoon*. His character is the avenging wraith which for the bulk of the film is someone with their face hidden under a helmet that does not speak, therefore, no need for Sheen to stick around. However, the character that Sheen represents does get a bit confusing and is a wobbly leg in the story.

Charlie Sheen arrives as the "new boy" in town named Jake. He has a specific set of scars on his back and neck. There are some flashbacks showing the murder of a local boy named Jaime who appears to have been slashed in those same places but who is not Charlie Sheen. Jake turns out to be the wraith, magically arrived to right the wrongs done to Jaime, and he IS actually Jaime. Why is he a different person though? He has the line, "this was as close as I could get," but it was still weird that he shows up to kill those who killed him wearing a different face. For story purposes, yeah, people would have recognized him had he shown up looking like himself but to that end: no need to BE the Jake character at all, could have shown up as the wraith, taken care of business, and then whooshed back off into the stars or wherever he came from.

One could argue that he was so in love with Keri, portrayed by Sherilyn Fenn, that he wanted to woo her all over again as Jake and be near her while he played his game with the gang members. Even with embracing the supernatural elements of the story the logic still is not adding up and for me when the magic killer who says he is Jaime but looks like Jake takes Keri away with him in the ending I was left thinking that it was a creepy move on his part and an odd one for her. Where are they going? Is he taking her to the land of the dead or what?

    The main villain is Packard played by Nick Cassavetes. I never would have recognized him with his hair. When I see the name of this actor I always picture him as the bald criminal Dietrich in the action movie *Face/Off*. Cassavetes is also an accomplished writer and director having been born into the business via his famous parents Gena Rowlands and John Cassavetes. In *The Wraith* he portrays a violent man who aside from harassing people on the roads is possessive of Keri. He has one of the most ridiculous lines of the film when he tells, threatens, Keri with the information that she belongs to him. He plays with his knife, forces Keri to cut his hand, but right before that he tells her how he feels with: "You and me we're like blood brothers. I guess you could call us blood lovers because of how much I love you." Weird. Keri makes it known that she has never had sex with him and never will. He disagrees.

    Keri is not willing to lay down with Packard but there is a scene where he is on top of a topless girl pawing at her. Keri also has her sex scenes, one in a flashback showing the time Jaime was pulled off of her to be murdered, and somehow she didn't realize who did that I guess. Then she has a topless, quite awkward makeout session with Charlie Sheen in a hot spring. Their relationship could have been developed better for sure. She rides on his bike once or twice and then he declares that he loves her and they get hot and heavy. She probably sensed he was Jaime and that drew her to him but maybe that could have been explored better.

Randy Quaid plays the lawman Loomis, Matthew Barry is Billy, Jamie Bozian Gutterboy, Griffen O'Neal is Oggie, and Chris Nash Minty but the standout cast member above all is Clint Howard, brother of famed director Ron Howard, as Rughead. What made his presence so wonderful? His hair! Clint Howard is a bald fellow but in this movie he has a big stack of hair on his head in the form of a wig that is paying homage to the lead character Henry from the 1977 David Lynch film *Eraserhead*.

All of the villains in this movie, even with the serious and dramatic situation they find themselves in, are quite zany and over-the-top. I kept thinking they belonged in a Police Academy movie instead. I am not complaining though, I do not think their style of presentation ruined the entertainment value of the film.

The special effects in the film are somewhat dated regarding the supernatural stuff but there is a comic book quality to those moments that "works." When the cars are racing there are some cool shots but also some sped up shots that make the action look sillier compared to more modern action films. This is no *Fast & Furious* and I thought it amusing that the illegal street racing gang always makes sure to put on their racing helmets before engaging in a race. The explosions are solid fun though with one car crash stunt involving a truck loaded up with cars having its load dumped being one highlight. The other stunt highlight to me was the explosion of the gang's garage hideout, it went BOOM real nice.

An action sequence that did not thrill me was when the wraith arrives at the garage of the gang and shoots the place up with a shotgun. The pacing and the music were both "off" to me and the scene does nothing but highlight the lack of logic for the entire story regarding how he plays with them instead of just getting justice. The way the gang members scramble for cover when the shooting starts though is funny.

"Who was that guy?"

"I don't know. But whoever he was he was weird and pissed off."

The music is grating in some spots yet cool in others. There is often an energetic composition being played that then has pipe organ sounds blared over it. Of course, there are songs on the soundtrack as well with the one I remember most being Billy Idol's *Rebel Yell*.

The wraith drives a futuristic car in the film as he races and kills the gang members. At the end of the movie Jake calls it a Turbo Interceptor but what the vehicle was in real life is a Dodge M4S. The car was designed to be used as a pace car in PPG-CART Indy Car races.

The Wraith is entertaining even with all of its flaws which makes me see it as a candidate for a cool remake. I am available for the gig, someone sort it out.

22. AFTER MIDNIGHT - 2019

After Midnight was written and directed by Jeremy Gardner, who also stars as the lead character Hank. This film is my first exposure to the arts crafted by Mr. Gardner. The directing credit is shared with Christian Stella.

The story introduces you to a loving couple through some flashbacks and then in the present the couple are going through some turmoil. Hank is alone in his rural house with his girlfriend having left him. After she leaves a monster starts visiting Hank's front door on a nightly basis attempting to claw its way in.

Abby is the name of Hank's girlfriend and it is Brea Grant acting out this end of the relationship across from Jeremy Gardner. I am not familiar with Brea Grant as an actor but she does a good job in this feature.

Jeremy Gardner as an actor, well, it took a while for me to settle in and roll along with his performance. It might not have been just him, however, perhaps it is the characters and the scene construction altogether that took a little bit for me to get comfortable in as a pairing, actors to scenes and dialog, overall flow. I'm saying I eventually found a comfortable float and enjoyed the acting and Indie tone.

An early critical thought I did have regarding this film involved the Southern location and characters. It sort of felt like hipsters playing as hillbillies instead of the genuine article. I could be behind in the hillbilly times though having left behind my own rural roots for a spell now. Perhaps they dress sharper these days with freshly pressed and clean country outfits. Yeah, Brea tells Hank that he is a "hunter" but when he goes off into the woods with his pal they look dressed for a fashion catalog, not getting down and dirty in the woods.

The timeline for the events in the movie felt a little askew. At first I had not realized that there was a ten-year gap between the first scenes we see of the couple and then the present when she has left but they do get around to clarifying that detail. However, if the beast began appearing the very day that Brea left then I do not understand how he went that long without getting any footage or pictures and just lived with a beast at his door nightly for that long; he says Brea was gone at least a month.

No one believes Hank and they all talk about him behind his back about how he is going crazy seeing monsters. Anyone who cared about him would have entertained the idea of staying with him to see the beast I think. The problem is, that even with some fantastical monster visiting his house, Hank himself is not even impressed or scared enough to alter his daily routine of moping about. Terror in the night but then he just forgets it and goes hanging out with pals and such talking about relationships.

If you are looking for a straight horror genre film then you might not dig the fact that the bulk of *After Midnight* is Indie relationship drama and analysis. Once the monster comes in for the final punchline of the film it is a lot of fun but also a very expected moment. I totally could tell that it was about to happen. It is satisfying but at the same time I ended up feeling like the entire movie gets reduced to being a buildup for a joke that could possibly have been told in a shorter format for mass appeal, a short or a meme. Maybe that is a weird saying that an enjoyable and cute movie might have made an even better meme in some way. I am shocked at myself, shame, shame, movie fan indeed.

After Midnight is a movie I liked and the horror angle provides a boost of creative originality to what could have been a run-of-the-mill relationship drama. The monster ends up being more silly than scary though.

23. WILLY'S WONDERLAND - 2021

The director of *Willy's Wonderland* was Kevin Lewis and the screenwriter was G.O. Parsons. I do not recognize either name or their previous works; however, there are lots of names I do not know and all that matters for this Hollywood story is that somehow Nicolas Cage saw the script and wanted to help bring it to life. Cage is one of the only actors in the industry who can pull off doing a horror movie like this and star in a blockbuster "big" film and no one will blink an eye at his creative choices. It is crazy how he is Hollywood's worst actor and quite possibly the best at the exact same time. Perhaps actors should watch Cage performances and take notes but if they try to emulate him more than likely they will come off looking silly. The career of Nicolas Cage is in many ways a more interesting, crazier-sounding story to me than a film where he is fighting animatronics possessed by the spirits of serial killers at a closed down restaurant.

I have read that the screenplay was discovered on the Blood List, somehow going from there to the eyes of Nicolas Cage. This list is similar to the Black List of Hollywood but with a focus on horror projects, ala a curated list of screenplays unproduced but liked by the person in charge of shaping the list. If I understand it correctly, the way to get a script on the list is to pay and submit it into a contest or something of that ilk. The way that Hollywood operates involves a lot of smoke and mirrors with a lot of the "made it" stories not being the whole truth. While keeping that in mind and knowing that people buy their awards and their stars on the Walk of Fame I do not want to bring up the Blood List as if I am advertising that writers should pay to enter contests. I would assume that nine out of ten times a screenplay contest is just a cash generator for whomever is pretending to read the scripts. Likewise, I am not making any negative claims about the Blood List and how it functions either, I do not know much about it just like I did not know the names of the creators of this film, I am clueless and instead of chasing screenplay contests saved my money to produce my own poorly received films.

    Originally titled *Wally's Wonderland*, *Willy's Wonderland* is different in many ways from *Five Nights at Freddy's* but it is impossible not to think that maybe somebody was trying to copy the story of that game. Now that *Five Nights at Freddy's* has its own movie series it will be interesting to see if producers plan to create a rivalry of sequel releases. *Five Nights at Freddy's* is a much slicker production with the Indie visuals of *Willy's Wonderland*, the less than inspiring camera work probably not going to be getting the job done in any popularity battle.

    Aside from Nicolas Cage the other main lead for the film is Emily Tosta as Liv. She is one of several teens who want to burn down the old restaurant because they know the adults in the community feed people to the animatronics to keep them from attacking the citizens of the area. I recognize Tosta from her role as Leticia in the television show *Mayans M.C.* I found her interesting in that show and interesting in this film and look forward to seeing her in more roles. I'm not sure her squaring off to fight stance translates all that strong on screen though.

Beth Grant is the sheriff in *Willy's Wonderland*. She is a face you might recognize from a slew of hit films even if you do not know her name like you do that of Nicolas Cage. *Speed*, *Donnie Darko*, and *Little Miss Sunshine* are a quick trio of title drops featuring Beth Grant.

The rest of the cast fill in roles of teenage victims and town residents in on the pact with the evil animatronics but those performances did not rise above the disposable characters that they were assigned. If you are looking for character depth there isn't too much to latch on to with this film in that regard; I guess Liv has the most fleshed out backstory meant to hold up that end of the film.

Mostly the movie is Nicolas Cage cleaning, drinking soda while he plays pinball, and then beating giant puppets to death in scenes cut and shot in a manner to try and inject energy into the action. All the energy comes from Cage himself—amusing, but the action itself is very lackluster.

The entire movie moves at an awkward pace and is filled with mundane montages of Nicolas Cage's mysterious Janitor character cleaning things or drinking soda. There is a late montage where he dances while playing pinball and it does indeed stand out as a grand highlight, perhaps the best moment of the entire movie because watching Nicolas Cage being quirky IS a treat.

By the way, Nicolas Cage doesn't speak in this movie. His character is silent and deadly, with some grunts and I think he did sort of whisper a few words at one point when unhappy with his pinball performance. Who the character is aside, from a drifter being tricked into cleaning the restaurant so that the animatronics might eat him, is left a mystery. It appears that drinking his brand of soda gives him super strength and that is amusing. I did not understand why he needed to also play pinball when he went to drink his sodas, however. In the middle of a fight if his watch timer went off to remind him to drink a soda he would also play pinball before returning, at one point he even left Liv to fend for herself so that he could take his "break." I guess it is just the way he is built. He isn't a hero in a classic sense.

When the Sheriff finds out that the animatronics are being defeated by the Janitor, instead of being happy that her town is being freed from a bloody curse she attempts to help the animatronics. This did not make any sense to me. Even after she handcuffs the Janitor and leaves him to die and he escapes and shows that he is a force to be reckoned with, instead of siding with him she still attempts to appease the leader of the killers, ala Willy the Weasel. I guess she could be that scared and maybe even a little warped but I just was not buying the logic.

A group of teens crash through the ceiling and get trapped in the restaurant. This is confusing because they just fell through a big hole in the roof, could they not climb some shelving and devise a way back out of said hole? Also, the Janitor character is shown to kick some doors right off their hinges. Maybe the chain on the front door is too tough for him to snap but surely the boarded-up windows would not have been a problem. I assume the rear exit was blocked or locked as well.

There are some mindless, goofy moments to embrace within *Willy's Wonderland*. The silliness of the animatronics and their profanity laced dialog is chuckle worthy. There are also some points of intrigue in the ending with a bigger story perhaps to be told involving the Janitor and Liv going on adventures. However, this is a B movie that for me doesn't rise above the pack with the constant montages, weak action sequences, and bland characters overall. It is the type of movie that needs the viewer to embrace the base premise with enthusiasm and bring their own positive energy to the viewing to pump things up. It is what it is and even if Nicolas Cage is a special talent he doesn't make it anything more, if that makes sense.

24. SCREAM - 1996

If there were a Mount Rushmore of horror directors then Wes Craven would be one of the first faces needing to be carved upon it. A master in the genre, one might say that he was put upon this Earth to inspire us via *A Nightmare on Elm Street*. While one of the Freddy movies was the first "adult" horror I dared to watch I think that because of my age at the time the first *Scream* movie is THE Wes Craven movie that struck me with bolts of creative energy. When it released it became a landmark moment in 90s cinema—even non-horror fans heard about the exciting event that the film became—at least it felt like the hottest thing going at theaters via word of mouth amongst kids my age. The *Scream* franchise is the one that I got to experience from the beginning as it was released; therefore, it holds a special place in the cinematic history files of my brain.

After its theatrical run I remember buying *Scream* on VHS at a Hastings store. I was raised by parents who only accepted full screen features and anything letterbox was inferior. No one had taught me about the benefits of viewing a movie in widescreen format and when I bought my *Scream* VHS I accidentally got the widescreen version. I popped the tape into my player and popped it right back out because having black sections at the top and bottom of the picture was unacceptable. I took the movie back to Hastings and asked to exchange it for a full screen version. This created an incident at the store because even though I had bought the movie from there in the first place the person I asked to exchange it for me checked my identification and was not willing to let me get an R-rated movie. I ended up getting a refund.

The quest to buy *Scream* continued at Walmart where I bought it and did not have any issues getting a copy. However, Walmart did refuse to sell me *The Craft* on VHS and I remember that well because the cashier made me embarrassed in front of other customers declaring that I was trying to buy an "adult" movie.

Kevin Williamson wrote the screenplay for *Scream*. His name is one of the first times where I can recall the name of a writer being a selling point. The writer is usually hidden in the credits but studios began to make sure that Williamson's name was out front after the smash success of *Scream*. I am familiar with many of his writing works but the two titles that I associate first and foremost are *Scream* and then the television show *Dawson's Creek*. Williamson had his finger on the pulse of "hip" pop culture at the time often incorporating a lot of pop culture references in dialog. As an aspiring writer it was cool to see not only a screenwriter getting marketing publicity, but that he was not just sealed into one genre right out of the gate with *Dawson's Creek* being a dramatic teen soap opera. Of course, the bulk of his credits are within the horror genre and it's not a bad way to make a living. Horror films can explore everything other genres offer and push past the edges of expectation into some bold, crazy territory.

Teens are stalked by a masked killer who makes a habit of calling to harass them on the phone with threats and horror movie trivia questions. It sounds like a basic setup but it is approached with the meta humor of knowing the history of such plots and the "rules" of horror movies. The film balances the comedic elements with a tragic heart when it comes to the killings and the drama in the lives of the characters. It is an intelligent slasher that slashed right into and shook up the genre. *Scream* can be taken seriously but one probably wouldn't say the same about the *Scary Movie* comedy horror franchise. *Scary Movie* is a slapstick, seriously goofy sendup of horror films and it spawned quite a few sequels. I bring it up because the original title of *Scream* was actually *Scary Movie*.

    A horror movie embracing "meta" content was not a new concept regardless of the kudos *Scream* gets for reinvigorating the horror genre in the 90s. Wes Craven must have had special interest in such projects because only two years prior to the release of Scream he wrote and directed the film *New Nightmare*. In *New Nightmare* the stars of Craven's *A Nightmare on Elm Street* franchise find themselves outside of the movie and seemingly being attacked by Freddy Krueger outside the films. Wes Craven even plays himself in the film.

    Drew Barrymore was already a "name" actor and it is said that she was approached to star as the leading lady Sidney in *Scream*. Instead, her star status gave the opening scene of the movie the shock value that helped create the buzz the film needed to generate enough sales in a year of blockbuster films to become the fifteenth highest grossing film. There doesn't seem to be any shortage of people taking credit for the idea of her being the first victim instead of the star with Barrymore herself saying it was her idea. In reading about the casting process, I think there is some between-the-lines truth about Barrymore not actually wanting to be a part of the film but also not wishing to irritate the intimidating producers, ala the Weinstein brothers—thus, she suggested herself for the Casey role instead of not coming to play at all.

    Neve Campbell is Sidney and she made it hers for sure; I can't imagine anyone else in the role. Her character's journey to let toughness counter her state of vulnerability in the face of fear mingled with past trauma is executed wonderfully. As the series has gone on she has not been as central regarding focus and I think the emotions and presence she brought into the first couple of stories were vital to their success.

    Skeet Ulrich matches very well with Neve Campbell in my opinion as her boyfriend Billy. Their relationship is going through some adolescent drama intensified by the fact that Sidney's mother was murdered; dead moms can't stifle a growing boy's raging hormones. I think their romance plays well in awkwardness and the drama value is strong when she cannot decide whether or not to trust him not to be the killer. Her instincts do turn out to be right and Billy is quite the emo psycho.

    The twisty ending revealing two killers was the perfect bookend for the opening of the film with a star actor being the first person to get brutally knifed. Matthew Lillard brought a lot of energy into the killer Stuart. It is a risky performance overall because his over-the-top quirks could have derailed the tone of the film but did not in my opinion. Wes Craven and company found the perfect balance with horror drama and comedy letting Lillard be silly yet taken seriously when it comes down to being a deranged lunatic and a threat. Some of his interactions with Randy, portrayed by Jamie Kennedy, show a bully side to the zany goof; a darkness just under the surface. Some of the best lines of dark humor in the ending sequences come from Stu as he worries about his parents finding out what he has been up to.

Rose McGowan plays Tatum, the best friend of Sidney. It is said that the production team envisioned her as a tomboy sort of character and McGowan rebelled against this and brought her own bright wardrobe and mannerisms to the character. She dates Stu in the film and they matched well in energy the same as Billy and Sidney I felt. The death of Tatum via getting crushed in a garage door while trying to escape via the doggy door portion of it might on the surface seem like a run-of-the-mill horror victim getting their number called for the body count. However, every single time I watch *Scream* I am rooting for her to make it through that door and for the outcome to be different for her.

David Arquette is another highlight of the cast as Deputy Dewey. He provides more comedy elements as a Barney Fife sort of deputy but his bravery and heart both pump strong. I have read that a version of the film was shot in which he and the Randy character both die but I think they made the right choice reversing those deaths and letting each of them live. The film originally got an NC-17 rating and aside from too many guts being shown and the stabbing of Casey being too brutal, it is said that the edited-out scene of Randy getting his throat cut was another too brutal for an R visual for the ratings board.

Courteney Cox as Gale Weathers is also interesting. She is a shark of a woman regarding thinking about her ratings and fame but then one gets to see that she is human after all in details such as her attraction to Dewey. For someone presented as somewhat adversarial she always comes through in the end as a willing hero.

Henry Winkler portrays the principal in this movie and is also known for famously portraying the character of Fonzie in the show *Happy Days*. There is a scene when the principal is being taunted by the killers with knocks on his office door. He tries to catch them in the act but the hallway is empty save for the janitor Fred. This moment is a spot where the movie goes a little too far I think with the meta content. The janitor named Fred is dressed similar to Freddy from *A Nightmare on Elm Street* and is recognizable as director Wes Craven.

A better cameo than that of the director Craven is the appearance of Linda Blair as a reporter. She should be known to horror genre fans as Regan in *The Exorcist.*

I loved *Scream* when it first came out but the one thing I would nitpick on was the death of Stu. He has a television dropped down on his face. It seems as though he smashes through the screen and gets electrocuted. I thought that it was a weak death and did not like it because I knew how hard it can be to break a television screen. I used to find old televisions left in a trailer park dumping ground as a teen and getting the glass to crack was a hard task.

In this viewing of the movie, I also cannot help but think that Billy and Stu drop the ball on all the work they have done by stabbing each other too early. They tell Sidney their plot and such, all in good villain fun, but why would they wound themselves BEFORE killing her and her dad? Why would they stab each other and then go about trying to stage bodies and kill folks? One can chalk it up to dumb teenagers getting ahead of themselves but it is another detail a critic could pick at I suppose. By the way, teenagers in the original *Scream* seem much older than the ones in some of the later films.

The iconic mask of the killer gets anyone who wears it in the series called Ghostface. Ghostface is often seen alongside genre legends such as Jason, Freddy, Chucky, and Michael Myers. I did notice in the movie that the costume package the cops end up getting in their investigation dubbed the mask as coming from a set for a Father Death costume. I think the first time I heard Ghostface mentioned is via Tatum when she sees it.

The song *Red Right Hand* by Nick Cave and the Bad Seeds has been used by other productions but in my head it is "the *Scream* song."

Scream has elements that over time are more obvious as flaws but it still remains a favorite of mine regarding the energy it sparked in my younger creative self which remains woven into the experience of every viewing.

25. SCREAM 2 - 1997

Wes Craven returned to direct, Kevin Williamson returned for the script, and the survivors of the first film returned for *Scream 2*. As a fan of the first film, I was happy to catch the newest installment at the theater opening weekend. I can remember leaving the showing a little disappointed but it wasn't really the movie's fault. I had a headache and the opening scene where the guy gets stabbed in the head did not make it feel any better. It is actor Omar Epps getting killed in a theater bathroom to open the film and I can recall, aside from the moment making my own headache hurt worse, being a critical teen scoffing at how well the blade went through the partition between the stalls. I also wondered how the killer had such perfect aim to go with that strength. I guess he could have been peeking over the partition a little.

Scream 2 might not have lived up to the initial hype I had going for it in my head back in 1997 but I have watched it quite a few times since then and I liked it much better without stabbing pain in my own head.

The opening scene victims are Omar Epps as Phil and Jada Pinkett Smith as Maureen. The scenario in which they are killed in a movie theater showing the movie version of the real crimes that took place within the first *Scream* film, is a creative setup that one could take as a statement about the glorification of crimes, or even on how we find entertainment in watching people being butchered. Maureen is stabbed to death in a crowded room yet no one notices at first. The killer blends in with all the other people in similar costumes going bonkers over the movie they are watching. However, when she stumbles before the big screen with such an expression of pain on her face and wails out in anguish, people then take notice and the concern on their faces I think actually shows how, as humans, we can balance entertainment with horror in it and not be monsters in reality when shown true pain and horror. Maybe I am being too silver-lining in my interpretation of empathy there but I grew up on violent movies and do not have any sort of disconnect from caring and I am optimistic that most can identify with that. Maybe the scene isn't meant to go that deep and is just a shock kill reminder about exploitation and sensationalization. I mean, the movie does end up having one of the killers make this his whole motive, ala he is going to say that watching movies turned him into a killer.

    I have read that when Kevin Williamson wrote the first *Scream* that he had treatments for sequels ready to go, pitching the concept as a franchise. Therefore, he was able to get to work quickly at penning out this sequel with ideas already in place to work from. However, it is also public knowledge that the screenplay leaked during production and some sources say the movie got late rewrites to change aspects in order to keep viewers in the dark. The movie came out the year after the first one; therefore, I am not sure how big the impact or delay really was involving the leaked script. Also, I have read other sources that imply that fake scripts were leaked on purpose to throw people off.

Scream 2 follows Sidney Prescott, Neve Campbell, to college where Jamie Kennedy as Randy is also going to school. Randy is not given as much screen time as the main characters of the film but it seems like maybe he still harbors a huge crush on Sidney and wants to be close to her to help protect her. It is a little side plot that could have been embellished I think some more, but Randy ends up on the chopping block and stabbed to death in the back of a van. As a survivor of the first film, it was probably a gut punch to some viewers but I think Randy himself explained that the rules were changed and no one was safe and it made sense.

I actually think Randy dying ends up following a little too safe and in line with rules. I mean, technically butchering Sidney in the middle of the movie would have been a bigger shocker. I am not saying that I would root for such a thing though, I like her character journey and rooting for Sidney is a large part of what makes this movie and the previous one satisfying.

I am not saying I was completely numb to Randy being offed. I do not find actor Jamie Kennedy all that funny in the part yet Randy seems to be trying to be funny quite frequently. I think that my NOT finding him funny makes him seem more like a real person to me in a weird way. So, yeah, Randy being killed was more impactful than many characters who are sacrificed to the genre blood gods.

The finger pointing and everyone is a suspect formula is a lot of fun in this sequel. However, as I watched and thought more about Randy laying out the anything goes rules for a sequel, it occurred to me that the elements that made the first *Scream* good were being revisited not rewritten completely. *Scream* is a movie that explores the rules of horror movies yet at the same time has its own little formula or rules going on for it.

    David Arquette returns as Dewey and he arrives at the college because he has seen on the news that some murders related to the *Stab* movie based on their ordeal have taken place. He arrives as another protector concerned for Sidney and it is cool how the survivors are a little family of sorts in that way. Gale Weathers, Courteney Cox, is present as well and it is fun seeing her and Dewey reunited. After they fell for each other in the first film it seems they had a falling out, but we get to see the same romance blossom once again and it is cute. Of course, Dewey then gets stabbed in front of Gale and it is heartbreaking. Lucky for Dewey his seeming to be dead but actually surviving is a joke the filmmakers ran with. Dewey surviving is another angle of comfort for fans similar to Sidney being able to fight and survive as well.

    Cotton Weary is a character from the first film who did not have a large part on screen but was a key player in the spider web of a plot. Liev Schreiber portrays Cotton who was framed for the murder of Sidney's mother and serving prison time for it in the first film; Billy and Stu actually killed the woman. It is interesting how they included him in the sequel as another player in the mix. However, he is not really a great guy. He seeks fame because he feels he is owed, but in the end when he is faced with either helping the killer or saving Sidney his hesitation just makes him seem even worse. I am somewhat reminded about Gale Weathers and her cutthroat way of doing things but when tested she does the right thing—with Cotton it felt like he had to be given an incentive to be the hero.

Jerry O'Connell plays Derek, the boyfriend to Sidney. It is a lot of twisted fun how they explore Sidney's trust issues and the psychological torture of having had a previous boyfriend turn out to be a psycho killer. Derek ends up getting shot to death and it is a brutal looking wound. As sad as it was to say goodbye to Randy I think Derek's death holds more emotional impact to me. I find it amusing to watch adult Jerry O'Connell and find that I am unable to shake away the image of the chubby little kid he was in the 1986 movie *Stand by Me*. He was one of the best actors in that movie as Vern.

Elise Neal portrays Hallie the roommate of Sidney. She is a supportive friend and as a new character provides a solid presence and is another example of someone getting knifed that you actually might care about a little bit. I am actually surprised that the body count for this film did not get a little higher. There are some cops killed as genre throw-a-way victims but if the filmmakers had wanted to get more bloodthirsty I think the sorority sisters portrayed by Rebecca Gayheart and Portia de Rossi had potential to be sliced and diced by Ghostface.

A college student who does get stabbed and then thrown off a balcony is Cici. Sarah Michelle Gellar is Cici and she had quite the decade in the 90s eventually becoming a household name as Buffy the *Vampire Slayer*. Gellar is also featured in the Kevin Williamson written horror movie *I Know What You Did Last Summer*. Her acting is on point in *Scream 2* and I really felt her character's fear over being alone in the sorority house as the killer threatened her over the phone.

Timothy Olyphant is Mickey, a film student and a part of Sidney's inner circle of friends. As a fan of *Natural Born Killers* I can appreciate the name choice for him though I guess they could have chosen it after Mickey Mouse or something. Olyphant has gone on to be quite the well-known actor but *Scream 2* looks like one of his first true leads and I think the manic energy he brought in is entertaining. He is not as quirky as Stu but in the end sequences when he is revealed to be the killer he explains himself with a lot of fun gusto.

The other killer turns out to be the mother of Billy from the first film. She met Mickey online when looking for a psycho to help her exact revenge against the woman who killed her son. Laurie Metcalf plays this character and I think she does a great job of being an unhinged madwoman with a knife in the end sequences. The duo chosen to be the killers were fun choices in my opinion. Billy's mother does make a comment that did not ring true to me, however. She tells Sidney she is the one who killed Randy. In the scene where Randy is killed the killer literally grabs him, lifts him up, and pulls/throws him into the rear of a van. I do not buy that Laurie Metcalf could have picked up Randy like that—it had to have been Mickey.

The end battle between Sidney and the killers takes place on a theater stage, again a nice full circle sort of bookend when considering the first scenes took place in a movie theater, and while the end results are satisfying the choreography in the battle is lackluster. After playing some darting around peek-a-boo with Mickey then Sidney runs around pulling levers and rattling sound effects in place for a play and this discombobulates Laurie

Metcalf's character. It is awkward to me.

 A fun fact that I will never forget about this movie is that in the opening theater scene the woman who hands Phil and Maureen their *Stab* prop costume was someone who won that role in a contest sponsored by MTV. MTV used to be cool. They used to mostly play music videos and I appreciate how much music they helped expose me to when I first got access to cable after my parents divorced.

 The soundtrack or *Scream 2* is one that I purchased with the first track *Scream* by Master P being all in good fun; uhhh. However, the rap group that I bought an album of after hearing them on the *Scream 2* soundtrack was Kottonmouth Kings. Their track *Suburban Life* is a good one from this movie but I found quite a few tracks to groove to on their Royal Highness album.

 Stab is the movie within a movie happening in *Scream 2* and the filmmakers did a good job of piling on to a joke from the first with one of the casting choices. In *Scream* Sidney makes the sarcastic comment that if they made a movie about her they would probably have Tori Spelling play her. In *Stab* within *Scream 2* Tori Spelling is indeed playing Sidney. Luke Wilson is Billy and his line "that's how the cookie crumbles" followed by him slapping himself in the head is hilarious; he does this while recreating the scene where Billy confronted Sidney about not being able to get over her mother's death to give him more lovin'. And then Heather Graham is Casey in the *Stab* reimagining of the opening scene from *Scream* that had Drew Barrymore in it.

 Scream 2 may not hold the same magic energy that the original managed to inspire me with but it is a solid sequel overall and rightfully solidified the property as franchise worthy.

26. SCREAM 3 - 2000

As my pal and I walked across the parking lot to the movie theater, eager to get inside to watch *Scream 3*, a large crowd from an earlier showing released out of the front doors of the building. There was youthful energy aplenty in that crowd with teenagers whooping and prancing toward vehicles. As we passed some fellows they yelled at us and what I thought I heard was something about "Romans." I shrugged it off.

The movie began and eventually a character named Roman came on to the screen and my pal and I looked at each other, suddenly the words in the parking lot were translated, the guy had yelled "Roman did it." Nothing in the plot of *Scream 3* really made up for the disappointment in sitting through the entire movie knowing that Roman was going to be the killer.

Wes Craven returned to direct *Scream 3* and once again the cast of characters that survived the original film reprised their roles as well. This time the story takes place in Hollywood where the latest *Stab* movie based on the killings started in *Scream* is experiencing some issues with a new set of murders halting production. At first the movie is in limbo just because someone is killing as Ghostface again but then the cats of the film start to get killed as well. Shenanigans abound as Dewey and Gale Weathers work with the actors portraying themselves and people they know to try and figure out who the new killer is.

Kevin Williamson did not return to pen the screenplay. It is said that he was too busy but left an outline for the new screenwriter to work from. Ehren Kruger, an interesting last name to pair with Wes Craven, was chosen to bring *Scream 3* to life but it sounds like things did not go smoothly and there is a lot of blame tossed around by those involved. I have read that Ehren ignored the outline and failed to capture the characters as they were in the previous films and thus Wes Craven and a slew of other people were constantly changing the screenplay well into shooting the film. It is also said that the studio forced the movie into the shape it eventually took due to the Columbine school shootings. The producers were afraid that a *Scream* movie would not be well received and it is said that they demanded the film lean more toward comedy and be less violent. In my opinion it is very noticeable that the tone of the film is "off." It is sort of like a wacky sitcom that got the beloved Scream character layered into it. As a Scream fan, because of my investment in caring about the characters, I find *Scream 3* watchable but not very likable. The first two films in the series are movies that I know by heart and can feel feeding my own creative energy when I watch them. I can never remember what happens to each character in *Scream 3* and the final half an hour or so is always somewhat new to me again. Maybe the film is far worse than I am giving it credit for and this is the way my brain deals with trauma.

Screenwriter Ehren Kruger's big writing credit before this film looks to have been the thriller *Arlington Road*. *Scream 3* does not seem to have been a major speedbump of any sort for his career. Kruger also has writing credits on The Ring, several *Transformers* films, *Ghost in the Shell, Dumbo,* and *Top Gun: Maverick.*

    The killer for the film, Roman, is portrayed by Scott Foley. His career is packed full of television roles and while I can't call him by name he is one of those faces that television fans probably recognize as someone different depending on what shows they binged. He does a solid job with the character and his motive is all in good fun as explained in the rules of how the third film in a trilogy will bring out something unknown from the past to flip the facts regarding what you thought you knew. It turns out Roman urged Billy and Stu on and was the "director" who pushed them into being murderers. He is a half-brother to Sidney who was abandoned by their mother after she ran away from Hollywood, having briefly pursued an acting career.

    There is a point in the story where Roman fakes his own death and is found stabbed in a coffin. Gale Weathers checks his pulse real quick and declares him to be dead. I can understand complaints from the fanbase as to how that all plays out. Even if the reasons for Roman being a killer are okay I think that him being the sole killer fell a little flat. Supposedly this dullness is another creation by the producers controlling what the filmmakers could craft thanks to the school shooting at Columbine. It is said that there was originally a second killer but because the school shooters were a duo the studio did not want to align with that number.

    From what I have read, Emily Mortimer as Angelina Tyler was supposed to be the second killer. She is the actor who is portraying the fictional version of Sidney for the *Stab* film and might have been a former classmate or something like that. Some fans do subscribe to the theory that Angelina was indeed the second killer in the film regardless of how it all ended up. The way she is killed offscreen and then her body is seen drug away doesn't prove that she was actually dead. Perhaps she escaped and is the first killer to have gotten away with their crimes? Of course, one would think her missing corpse would have come up in the aftermath at some point if that is true. One could also believe she was the second killer but Roman double-crossed and killed her as well.

    The schedules of the main cast are another excuse given when the quality of *Scream 3* is discussed. I noticed that a lot of time was being spent with new characters or Gale and Dewey instead of the real heart of the franchise Sidney. Never Campbell was apparently busy and could only fit in so many days on the shoot, therefore, Sidney's scenes are more limited even while the movie circles around still being about her journey and coping with the psychological fallout of constantly being a "final girl" type. When she arrives in Hollywood I felt a tone shift back toward the previous films but it did not last. It seems like this third film was meant to be the end of the series and they did do a nice job of giving Sidney a satisfying happy ending.

    Cotton Weary, Liev Schreiber, doesn't get a happy ending or *Scream 3* beginning really. Kelly Ruthford plays his girlfriend Christine and the couple are the opening victims of the film. It is a solid enough opening I think and Cotton made for a good target having been not the greatest person in the previous film. The opening does introduce the fact that the killer is now using a voice changer that can mimic the voices of other people though and this aspect of the film is kind of goofy. It really gets stupid I think when the killer is taunting Sidney with the voice of her dead mother. While being taunted by the voice of one's dead mother does sound upsetting, it is not my favorite addition to the sense of reality laid down by the previous films.

While I do not think that the *Scream* elements fit perfectly with the comedy formula I also have to admit that some of the comedy bits do get me to chuckle. Dewey having to hang around with Gale and the actress playing the fake version of Gale is a solid comedy arrangement in general. Parker Posey portrayed Jennifer Jolie the actress playing Gale in the *Stab* movie within the movie. I think she is an interesting actor in general and one of her funniest moments is at the end of a scene when she is left alone with her bodyguard and she hops up into his arms for him to carry her. The bodyguard is portrayed by Patrick Warburton and his presence doesn't help steer things away from having a sitcom vibe because as someone that grew up watching *Seinfeld* I recognized him as Elaine's boyfriend David Putty.

Patrick Dempsey plays Mark Kincaid the homicide detective that becomes a romantic interest for Sidney. I think that his character and inclusion is solid and that his partner portrayed by Josh Pais is humorous as well. The character portrayed by Pais probably should have gotten some sort of death or movie exit but he just kind of vanishes from the story at some point. I have read that the Kincaid character also vanished in an original draft and they re-shot the ending of the movie to include him because the action was too lackluster with Sidney defeating Roman rather easily.

Silly celebrity cameos include the characters Jay and Silent Bob interacting with Gale as they pass her on a studio tour and then Carrie Fisher is a record keeper at the studio who looks suspiciously like Carrie Fisher of *Star Wars* fame to Gale though she is actually a failed actress named Bianca.

Famed B movie producer Roger Corman has a cameo in a scene where he explains how the studio needs to distance themselves from the violence in the news and therefore the Stab movie needs to be put on hold. Lance Henriksen is involved in this decision as the producer character John Milton and I think that this scene is Wes Craven and company getting meta on their experience trying to make *Scream 3* while facing pressure from the executives due to the school shooting.

The character of John Milton gets his throat cut by Roman who wishes to pin the death on Sidney. In the movie Roman is directing ala real life, he plans to get away with the murders. Milton is the movie producer from the 70s who threw a wild party at which it sounds like Sidney and Roman's mother got raped thus changing her and the course of all their lives. There is a chance that along with commenting on how real-life violence was ruining their movie production that this character was meant as a reflection of one of the film's real producers, Harvey Weinstein. Harvey held a lot of power in Hollywood for a long time and it was apparently a not so well-kept secret that he would pressure actresses into sleeping with him or in some cases outright rape women. People finally got together and worked to get charges placed against the man and the guilty verdicts in his trials have gotten him some double-digit prison sentences to serve.

Jamie Kennedy's character Randy died in *Scream 2* but they bring him back on a videotape in *Scream 3* to talk about the rules for a horror trilogy. A section explaining "the rules" is a solid addition but the fact that Randy would have recorded a tape prior to his death and on it stating, "if you are watching this I didn't survive," is kind of dumb to me. He made the tape not only in case of him getting killed in *Scream 2* but also assuming that the killers would be caught and that his friends would survive and find themselves in a third film scenario. It is a poor stretch of logic just to bring back the fan favorite character.

The signature phone voice for Ghostface in the *Scream* films is provided by a man named Roger Jackson. *Scream 3* had him in place along with a lot of the original winning elements regarding talent, but they still goofed around with it all too much and this third film is weak even if it did serve up that happy ending for Sidney, which I would have found acceptable enough had this been the final movie in the franchise. This film does make it seem like the property had run its course.

27. SCREAM 4 - 2011

It took eleven years for a new *Scream* movie to get released after fans were told the property would end as a trilogy. *Scream 4* saw Wes Craven and Kevin Williamson reunited as a creative force to see if they could recapture the same magic that they captured in 1996. It would prove to be the final film directed by Wes Craven before a brain tumor ushered him into death in 2015. And it sounds like the studio powers swooped in to meddle with the creative process, to some degree hijacking the grand hopes the creators and fans had for *Scream 4*.

Kevin Williamson wrote a screenplay for *Scream 4* but I have read at least eight writers dabbled on the material with the same screenwriter that did not impress with *Scream 3*, Ehren Kruger, being among them. In my opinion the most glaring issues with *Scream 3* and *Scream 4* that show off the fact that Williamson was not the final word in the process is the way the comedy is handled. The person trying to balance the elements drags their leg too deep into cornball humor and doesn't give the drama more room to express some heart and depth. The basic horror elements of a killer killing work fine but the movie is "fine" without impact.

Neve Campbell, Courteney Cox, and David Arquette all returned for this film, and as a fan I missed them and enjoyed seeing them. I was ready for a sequel, hungry for more Scream, excited for the possibilities. The characters of Sidney, Gale, and Dewey are mostly there to elicit nostalgia from OG fans and just "go through the motions" more than not. They do work well as the driving force behind what ends up being the punchline of the film concept with this story investigating the rules of horror remakes or reboots. It looks like the torch is being passed to a younger cast but then Sidney gets to close the curtains with the line "Don't fuck with the original." Applause for that.

    The opening of *Scream 4* is a fun one with different celebrities acting out scenes from the movie within a movie *Stab* series as it is being watched by what ends up being the real opener victims, Jenny and Marnie portrayed by Aimee Teegarden and Britt Robertson, knifed by Ghostface. The character of Marnie is killed offscreen and then lifted up and thrown through a door, crashing through the glass and wood which made me think: this Ghostface is going to be a strong person. However, when the killers are revealed it reminds me of how in *Scream 2* Billy's mother pretending to be a reporter named Debbie Salt took credit for killing Randy, but the person who killed him lifted him right off of his feet; she wasn't exactly a big strong woman, and my disbelief couldn't be squashed.

    Dewey is now a Sheriff and his entire force of officers are crafted in his somewhat bumbling mold. In *Scream 3* Dewey is not the sharpest tool in the shed but he did have the one moment where he saved Gale by shooting Ghostface and it was a flash of skill to match his genuine bravery. In *Scream 4* he just gets to show up late and pull some faces of reaction and in the end gets himself hit in the head with a bedpan. The way the police in this movie are all idiots is one of my biggest complaints about the humor style for the film. Marley Shelton portrays one of the main deputies Judy Hicks with Anthony Anderson and Adam Brody also being deputies given some key screen time.

Alison Brie is Rebecca Walters, the agent helping Sidney on her book tour; Sidney is promoting an inspirational book in this film, having returned to her hometown for that purpose. This is another character who just comes across as another clone trying to be like Gale Weathers in professional attitude, at least the way Gale seemed to be in the early going of the series; there are a lot of selfish fame seekers in the Scream franchise I suppose. I like Alison Brie as an actor but her character did not add to anything but the body count.

The best character in *Scream 4* is Kirby as portrayed by Hayden Panettiere. She has some firecracker energy. I am glad that even though it seems like she gets killed in this movie she actually survives to return in later sequels.

Rory Culkin is Charlie Walker in *Scream 4* and is indeed a sibling of the *Home Alone* star Macaulay Culkin. His character is a film buff incel who has lost his patience with women not giving him attention. It is really easy to buy into him as one of the psycho killers, extra scary perhaps to people who find human horror villains more terrifying than supernatural ones, because there seems to be a lot of these kids out there letting cheesy Internet philosophies guide them into becoming weaker and more prone to acting out in tantrums of violence.

Emma Roberts is Jill Roberts and is the other half of the killing duo for *Scream 4*. She is related to Sidney and wants her shot at fame with her motive being to become the new Sidney and famous. She delivers her motive in a preachy diatribe, but I think she was a fun choice as a killer and the "preachy" confessions are a part of the *Scream* franchise in general. When she sets about wounding herself to make herself seem like the sole survivor I think Emma Roberts let out an admirable scream of pain and her frustrated kicking of a table after the stab wound was good stuff.

      The *Stab* films are a fictional horror franchise that exist int he *Scream* movies as fictionalized takes on the murders that occur. The footage for the original *Stab* was said to have been shot not by Wes Craven but rather director Robert Rodriguez. Rodriguez is responsible for the *Spy Kids* movie series but is no stranger to horror having directed *From Dusk Til Dawn* and *Planet Terror*. When the Stab footage appeared in the previous Scream films no credit was given to Rodriguez; however, during the *Stab* film party in *Scream 4* when the movie is being shown a director's credit for Rodriguez appears on the screen; this is the footage with Heather Graham portraying the Casey character made famous by Drew Barrymore.

      There is a scene where Sidney is being attacked by Ghostface. I thought it was both killers with how the killer would pop up at each door. Soon after this attack Charlie and Jill are both shown to be hanging out at Kirby's house and I was wondering if the timeline of the film might have gotten a little messed up. I wasn't sure how either killer could have been attacking Sidney and then just be chilling at Kirby's house shortly thereafter. The entire scenario of the teens constantly leaving their homes to hang out felt a little odd too, not sure they would have been so keen to tempt fate. Kirby and Jill seem to get over having seen their friend butchered a few scenes previous a little too easily. Well, obviously Jill did because she is one of the killers but it is just more food crumbled onto my thoughts while watching where I thought about the tone "balance" not being perfect.

At one point Kirby and Sidney are running together and Kirby informs Sidney that they can lock themselves in a room downstairs for safety. They enter the room, lock the door, and then it is shown that one wall of the room is windows with doors to the outside of the house. How was that a safe room to run and hide in?

Visually *Scream 4* is often blurry, lights often making scenes fizzy with actors having that fuzzy glow around them. I am not sure who or what is to blame for that but I wasn't a fan of this look.

Scream 4 is not a complete return to glory for the series. However, it is an entertaining enough experience and has a cute ending.

28. SCREAM - 2022

In my first *Horror Movies Binge* book I watched a lot of the *Friday the 13th* films and I was not critically kind to them. As the end credits rolled on my latest viewing of *Scream*, the fifth entry in the *Scream* franchise not the first of the same title, I thought about how dumb I considered the *Friday the 13th* films and how the *Scream* franchise might be considered just as dumb by someone else. I think that even the worst of the *Scream* series is at least entertaining in a mindless "go with the flow" way. Perhaps this is generational perspective and exposure, I grew up with *Scream* more than I did *Friday the 13th*, and I see *Scream* as an evolution and improvement for the slasher genre over the exploits of Jason Vorhees. Of course, being meta commentary on horror films in general, the *Scream* movies gave themselves a bit of an "out" for critical analysis of their flaws and one can go with the flow with any film if they choose to. I guess I want to say that even when I blast something as being dumb I understand those dumb films have a strong fanbase who love them and THAT is not dumb. Fandom and horror sequels are at the forefront of *Scream* regarding the motives of the killers, so, I see why I am musing over what I am musing over. I like the idea of *Friday the 13th* in a historical sense but actually sitting through the old films is torture for me. But bring on the *Screams*!

Why is *Scream 5* actually titled just *Scream*? Because it is a re-quel! A re-quel is a blend of a reboot and a sequel for a film franchise, an attempt to make something new but keeping it connected to the past features so as not to anger the original fanbase that supported the franchise into success. Thus, *Scream* explores the "passing of the torch" to a new, younger cast while making sure that Sidney, Dewey, and Gale as the stars from the previous films are also given plenty to do in the feature. They nailed the meta spirit I think and *Scream* is quite clever.

First and foremost, I think *Scream* is going to be remembered most for being the one in which Dewey is killed. The scene is a gut punch for fans of the character because Dewey surviving has always been a pillar of franchise comfort. Initially I was right there with the fans who think that this death did not need to happen. However, this subsequent viewing of the film made me appreciate the moment more. The kill itself is quite the brutal statement with Dewey getting a knife stabbed into his back and his front which the killer then lifts and cuts through him ensuring no survival. It is a tragic end for the bumbling yet brave lawman and it works regarding giving this movie more emotional depth. Dewey is dead and gone and I think that the energy of that heartbreak transfers over into rooting for the rest of the "good guys" to overcome the killers; helps set up some of the younger characters as being just as memorable and worthy of rooting for as Sidney and company from the original.

Dewey isn't the only returning cast member who has run out of lives. Judy Hicks, actor Markey Shelton, from *Scream 4* is now the Sheriff and she gets stabbed to death right in front of her house. The scene doubles down on brutality with her son Wes, actor Dylan Minnette, getting killed inside of the house shortly thereafter. Wes is stabbed ever so slowly into and through his throat. This character seems to have been named after the departed Wes Craven and his death sets up a scene later on where characters can give a toast to him by name and in a way it is a toast to the director who guided the first four films of the franchise. For the toast scene many of the actors from previous *Scream* movies actually have their voices inserted into the crowd stating, "To Wes." At the end of the movie there is also a dedication to Wes.

    The *Scream* of 2022 was written by James Vanderbilt and Guy Busick. The writing credits of Vanderbilt are not genre confined, *Zodiac*, *White House Down*, *The Amazing Spider-Man 2*, but it does look like his first feature credit was indeed in the horror genre with the 2003 film *Darkness Falls*. Guy Busick wrote some episodes of *Stan Against Evil* and was also a writer on the 2019 horror romp *Ready or Not*.

    A duo of directors helmed *Scream*: Matt Bettinelli-Olpin and Tyler Gillett. This directing duo also directed the aforementioned film that Guy Busick wrote for: *Ready or Not*. It is easy to see how they got this directing gig if you have seen *Ready or Not* regarding entertaining energy being artistically captured.

    There is some humor present in this *Scream* but unlike the last two installments I think that the balance was once again achieved. The dramatic elements provide emotional connection and the horror elements are dark and brutal. When people get hurt in this film you can see the pain on their faces and feel their agony. I have read that Wes Craven had a really hard time getting blood and gore past the ratings board with the previous *Scream* films but the filmmakers here seem to have gotten far more brutal and personal feeling blade work approved. The blood gushes with a chord of authenticity and every single stab is intense.

The gag in the movie that made me laugh is a simple interaction between a boyfriend and girlfriend when the girlfriend is ready for the boy to take her upstairs for some sexy time. Mason Gooding is the character Chad and he is making out with Liv portrayed by Sonia Ammar. Liv is ready to have sex but Chad declines her invitation and tells her it is because he is not 100% sure that she isn't the killer. Liv was insulted and I was amused.

The Chad character has a sister in the form of Mindy who is portrayed by Jasmin Savoy Brown. Chad and Mindy are the children of Martha Meeks who is portrayed by Heather Matarazzo. Martha popped up in *Scream 3* as the sister of Randy who died in *Scream 2*. I think the siblings Chad and Mindy did a solid job as characters paying homage to Randy and being fun to root for as survivors.

Neve Campbell as Sidney and Courteney Cox as Gale take on the role of Ghostface hunters in this film. In the end they get to team up to take out one of the killers and Sidney is given another fun line just like in *Scream 4* letting the killers know what she thinks about their horror movie plans. One of the killers in this film talks about how the torch must be passed on. After the killer gets lit on fire Sidney states: "Enjoy the torch." It is as solid a punchline as the "don't fuck with the original" line from *Scream 4*. However, this *Scream* does an even better job with the witty one-liners in the end also giving the Tara character the chance to comment on her preference for more cerebral or "intelligent" horror films. She puts a bullet into the head of a killer and then states, "I still prefer the *Babadook*."

The character Tara is portrayed by Jenny Ortega and I really enjoyed her performance. I think what it is the softness in her voice when she delivers certain lines that really made her acting standout. She is also blessed with some big eyes that sell emotion easily enough on camera.

Tara's older sister Sam is set up as the new leading lady hero ala the new generation of Sidney. She is portrayed by Melissa Barrera and while some early scenes of her being upset made me think the acting might be too soap opera in style I think the performance leveled out and by the end she walks the walk and talks the talk of a badass to root for. Her character is interesting in that she is the daughter of serial killer Billy from the first film and she sees him, actor Skeet Ulrich, in visions coaching her to embrace her inner psycho. The "ghost of Billy" element could easily have been too silly an inclusion here, but I think the filmmakers managed to pull it off and it added another element of fun to the formula. When Sam goes to town stabbing the final killer with a knife it is a crazy, bloody mess to witness and the viewer is given the opportunity to root for a hero to "go mad" in the moment.

The killers in *Scream* are perhaps the least interesting aspect. Jack Quaid is Richie, the boyfriend of Sam and then Mikey Madison is Tara's friend Amber. Their motive for the killings is all about making sure the *Stab* movie franchise resets itself to better appease fans who were unhappy with the latest sequel ala *Stab 8*. Their motive is silly yet does fit with the *Scream* franchise in general. Perhaps these killers are not meant to be as interesting as some of the previous ones which fits with the ending in which Gale talks about not wanting to write a new book involving their crimes because they need to just die off without any fame for their murderous misdeeds.

The killer Amber takes credit for the killing of Dewey. I do not know if this is being done on purpose at this point but this kill marks another moment where I am not buying that the petite killer pulled off the kill. Amber overpowered Dewey and cut him in that lifting of the blades manner?

Another curious thing about the Amber character is that Mikey Madison is also in the Quentin Tarantino film *Once Upon a Time in Hollywood*. In that movie her character gets beaten and set on fire while screaming. In *Scream* she gets set on fire and then comes screaming back into the room and I am wondering if this was done on purpose or just coincidence that the same actress met similar fates in different films.

They did a great job with *Scream 5* regarding tone and horror entertainment value. It is not an easy thing to churn out sequels in a horror franchise without going off the rails with box cars full of garbage but the filmmakers did a bang-up job revitalizing the spirit of the franchise in brutal fashion.

29. SCREAM 6 - 2023

Witty stupidity.

The directors of *Scream,* ala *Scream 5,* returned for *Scream 6* as did the screenwriters and the surviving cast from the prior film, with the leading character Sam also still talking to her dead serial killer dad Billy, ala Skeet Ulrich; I said survivors and felt I needed to point out that a dead character returned as well. Billy is not the only returning dead character either! Kirby, actor Hayden Panettiere, is revealed to have survived being stabbed by Charlie in *Scream 4* and is now an FBI agent. Some of the new cast members included Dermont Mulroney, Josh Segarra, Jack Champion, Liana Libnerato, and Devyn Nekoda.

I thought that *Scream 5* brought a lot of fresh energy to the franchise and was a dark treat. *Scream 6* manages to keep that same tone and is slick to watch, but I also felt like I was watching something in which the creative process was wobbly, big productions bring in a lot of people with a lot of ideas to juggle and I felt like I could sense the problems within the circus.

First off, I was able to guess who the killer was as soon the character Quinn, Liana Liberato, mentioned she had a dead sibling. Someone who is not a fan of the previous films or as up to speed on lore might not catch the cookie crumb there but it just clicked for me right away. Quinn's dad is a police officer, Dermont Mulroney as Detective Bailey, therefore, I assumed that he was involved. This was made too clear when Sam tells him about her therapist and then right after that Ghostface chooses to kill her therapist. So, when Quinn dies in the film I knew it was another trick like with Roman from *Scream 3* and her cop dad was able to cover it up/fake the death. The third killer for this is Quinn's brother portrayed by Jack Champion and called Ethan. I cannot say that I knew he was going to be a killer but really the wind was already out of the sails early on for me to care.

    Watching the movie while having already guessed who the killers are is not that bad. It is still an entertaining ride. However, once I have picked a hole in one thing my mind is prone to picking at and chipping off more flakes regarding the Hollywood paint of the art. The *Scream* series often involves pacing issues as characters try to elude Ghostface and those were strong here in my opinion. The final showdown is a little awkwardly paced with their scrambling to get away and such. However, the scene that bugged me the most is the one in which Ghostface is trying to break into a room while the characters are using a ladder to go out of the window. The tension failed to manifest for me and I thought it felt oddly drawn out how many times the killer banged against the door trying to move the dresser blocking it before eventually getting inside.

    Skipping ahead to the ending once again, seeing as I already told you who the killers are too, the character Tara, Jenna Ortega, gets stabbed in the back and then runs around like nothing happened. I chalked it up to adrenaline and basic horror fun. However, she then gets viciously stabbed in the stomach as well and after the killers are defeated she is super chill and hanging out.

Instead of going to get help for their wounds and others Tara and Sam decide to sit and have a talk.

Another aspect from the previous films that should have been avoided is having a smaller killer taking credit for some physical feats I couldn't buy into. Petite killers lifting people up and throwing them around is not needed. Quinn in this film joins that list when she kills Gale's strong looking boyfriend. Sure, a small person could ambush and kill someone easy enough, but then she like throws his body into the room and I think it takes an extra notch out of the believability of the story that is already amusingly convoluted and in need of a lot of logic suspension. This aspect does not kill the fun, just as an outsider looking in, easier to judge from this vantage point, just another frayed end that could have easily been clipped.

Samara Weaving stars in the horror film Ready or Not that was also directed by Matt Bettinelli-Olpin and Tyler Gillett. She opens *Scream 6* as a teacher being hunted by Ghostface. The opening is some twisted fun with two killers that also get killed. If someone thinks it is a little too intricate and goofy I would not fault them though. I really loved the line delivered by Ghostface, however, as he slashes the guy who kills Weaving's character to death: "Who gives a fuck about movies?" This moment in the opening mentions finishing Richie's film, one of the killer's from *Scream 5,* and is perhaps one of the too early clues putting a viewer's mind on to connecting the dots regarding motives; relatives out for revenge is not a new thing for the *Scream* films.

For the most part the cast in *Scream 6* does a great job and I would be sure to check out any of the survivor's adventures should they be the focus of a sequel. I do have to say though that I don't feel like Courtney Cox has really been bringing the heat as Gale Weathers for the last few appearances. In close shots of Gale holding a phone her hands were creepy to me. I know, I am being a weird and shallow people-watcher on that comment. Also, it was great to see the character of Kirby again but something was off in that performance as well. I know the actor was returning from a long-acting hiatus but I think what might have been throwing me was something visual: her hair. Something was off about her hair. Movies are a visual medium I suppose and every human will be drawn to or turned off by different things.

    Neve Campbell did not return as Sidney and it was because she felt that the pay being offered to her was an insult. She decided what she felt her value was to the franchise and stood her ground. I applaud that but I also think that the series lessened the need for her by the third film even if she served up the punchline about her franchise OG status in the fourth film.

    Sam stabbing the last killer in the eye is a satisfying punctuation mark at the end of the fight. I think that Sam as a hero dealing with psychotic mental issues and perhaps some violent cravings is the type of hero the genre deserves; a beautiful thing.

    Scream 6 has orchestration issues that bugged me too much in this my second viewing but there were still some really fun horror moments making it a solid addition to the franchise. Keeping a franchise of films alive and of quality is not an easy task and even with my complaints *Scream 6* keeps my hope alive for more sequels.

30. THE LAST VOYAGE OF THE DEMETER - 2023

Norwegian filmmaker Andre Ovredal directed *The Last Voyage of the Demeter*. Some of his prior films include *Trollhunter*, *The Autopsy of Jane Doe*, and *Scary Stories to Tell in the Dark*. As a little kid I would check out the *Scary Stories to Tell in the Dark* books from the school library every chance that I got. I can also recall that after my parents divorced and my brother and I were meeting the "new guy" that would become our stepdad, one of the first outings involved going to the shopping mall and he gave us some cash to go shop with while he and Ma got some alone time. I bought a *Scary Stories to Tell in the Dark* book from Waldenbooks. Of course, none of that has anything much to do with the movie *The Last Voyage of the Demeter* but it is a movie that didn't keep my mind from wandering.

First the positive: the production value is there visually regarding setting and atmosphere. Also, the cast are excellent in their roles even if I think their characters are dumb fodder for Dracula to feast on and not much more. Corey Hawkins is the lead as Clemens and he does a fine job with Aisling Franciosi, Liam Cunningham, and David Dastmalchian also being strong performers on the cast.

Second the negative: I hated every second of this story as it unfolded. *The Last Voyage of the Demeter* did nothing but test my patience and annoy me. This movie takes the genre trope of wanting to yell at characters not to be so dumb to new levels. I mean, they know there is a killer picking them off one by one but they spend a lot of time trying to ignore it and then just doing other stuff in the daytime other than hunting the thing down and killing it. Sure, there are some scenes with them looking around the ship but it doesn't come across as such an expansive vessel that they could not have found what they were looking for. Add to this that at one point they find the crate Dracula sleeps in and even state: we have found where he sleeps. So, why didn't they try to catch and kill him in his sleep the next day? Instead, they concoct a stupid plan to wound him and sink the ship.

The movie opens with words on the screen explaining the story and what will happen. After you read that the opening scenes pretty much repeat what you just read. Why watch the movie when you know everything already? The creative material used to fill in what goes down is not interesting at all. Strong sailors bicker a little and then get killed in a dull game of Dracula and mouse. I found it odd that none of the men really did much fighting back when attacked by their killer. Yeah, there is resistance in the final showdown scenario but all the boring time spent before is basically Golem from *The Lord of the Rings* movies having his way with them.

Dracula is in beastly/demonic form in this movie and that is cool in some shots. When he is standing still and posing for some shots he is indeed creepy. However, for the bulk of the film you are getting a generic looking CGI animated creature void of any scary realism.

This movie does not have an ending! After you spend your time giving the movie the benefit of the doubt that maybe it will surprise you in the end all that you are rewarded with is that the entire movie is someone's attempt at an opening for a series of films featuring a surviving character, Clemens, wishing to hunt down Dracula. By the way, Clemens got his throat cut open by Dracula and then in the final shots it looks like he did not need to treat the wound or that it just vanished. I should have expected an insulting cliffhanger instead of an ending I suppose. I doubt there will be more films and if there are I will not support them; fool me once, my last voyage indeed.

31. VIDEODROME - 1983

The films of David Cronenberg somewhat defy genres with the filmmaker exploring horror, science fiction, action, and drama with a unique vision that one could just call the Cronenberg genre. "Body horror" is the genre label that is generally pinned to the works of the director due to his indulgence in making audiences squirm while the human form is manipulated, perverted, or harmed. *Videodrome* is considered one of his early body horror films. Cronenberg wrote and directed the film and while it was not a smash hit upon release, it grew as a film with a cult following and eventually became considered by many to be a classic. The Criterion Films Collection is picking classics, right? I watched this on a Criterion 4K movie release that is cool in that the case is designed to look like an old VHS tape. And calling it a film with a "cult" following is a good choice of words because the film gives you the fun mantra of "Long live the new flesh."

James Woods stars in *Videodrome* as Max Renn. Max runs a small cable television station that seeks to give audiences alternative programming ala pornographic and violent offerings. A man named Harlan, actor Peter Dvorsky, pirates some footage from a show called *Videodrome* and shows it to Max. The show appears to be snuff footage of people being tortured and murdered yet Max is inspired by it and thinks that it might just be the future of entertainment. He is convinced that he needs to buy this show for his cable station when the woman he is dating, Nicki Brand, shows that she is really turned on and fascinated by the program as well. Max's investigation into the origins of the show uncover that it involves a broadcast signal that can warp a person, ala they grow what is either a brain tumor or a new organ and start seeing reality in a different way, ala hallucinations. The people who created *Videodrome* have a plot to unleash it upon the world and Max becomes not only their latest test subject but someone they can program to do their bidding regarding positioning *Videodrome* for a successful launch. Or is Max just hallucinating?

    Debbie Harry plays the role of Nicki Brand in this movie and it is an interesting casting choice because I do not really associate her with acting. Debbie Harry is possibly best known as being the lead singer of the band Blondie who had the smash hit song *Heart of Glass*. She does a solid job and her presence really adds to the aesthetic of the film's tone. It is an edgy character that has a taste for pain along with their kink. In a sex scene she tests Max's own desires by having him pierce her ears during the act. Someone getting their ear pierced doesn't seem all that awful but when you pair it with sex it becomes rather creepy—well, to me, perhaps it is your own fetish and I am a vanilla puppy.

    James Woods in the acting department on this is a passing grade as well. He does some facial expression when trying to express emotion that do not land as real but overall, it is easy to buy into him as the conflicted cable television station manager who lets his curiosity take him too far down the rabbit hole. Woods has had a long acting career and his performances in *Salvador* and *Ghosts of Mississippi* both landed him Oscar nominations, however, when I think of him my brain sees him in only three films: *Videodrome, The General's Daughter*, and *Vampires*.

As I write this I think that James Woods is less known for acting and more known for his pushing Republican party political talking points on social media. He has been involved in some quirky lawsuits surrounding social media, suing others over what they have posted and having himself sued for things he has posted. Another lawsuit that I think is interesting involved actress Sean Young in the late 80s. Woods is said to have sued her and accused her of stalking him after they starred in the movie *The Boost* together. Young countered that Woods was just miffed that she declined his own advances toward her when they worked together. The case was settled out of court.

Other *Videodrome* cast members include Sonja Smits, Jack Creley, Lynne Gorman, and Leslie Carlson. Mr. Carlson is especially creepy in the film as Barry Convex, the man supposedly in charge of getting *Videodrome* out to unwitting consumers. I once had a school teacher who kept calling me Leslie even though I obviously was writing the name Wesley on my papers. Also, I once worked with a guy for a couple of years who thought my name was Wendell and he was pretty miffed when he found out I was not named that and had never corrected him.

Renowned special effects master Rick Baker headed up the special effects department for *Videodrome*. There are pulsating video tapes and televisions and Max's torso opens up to become a slot of tapes and other items, while his hand becomes fused to a gun; a gooey weapon having spent some time inside of that opened torso slot as well. The effects for the film do not look realistic but I think they still have the power to gross out or intrigue plenty of viewers.

    The movie explores humans and their consumption of media as well as sexual desires and our primal connections to violence. I think that the theme of humans and technology hits the mark regarding how Cronenberg explores our evolution, for better or worse, probably much worse, into seeing reality differently due to the tech. In *Videodrome* it is assumed that the future of humankind is to live more through our televisions or blend our reality with that fiction as characters with even panhandlers standing on street corners with televisions offering to let you get some screen time for some spare change. This vision is not that far off really and perhaps people of the 90s and early 2000s who were fans of the movie saw reality shows and such as the prophecy being fulfilled. However, I think that while the movie is on the mark with what technology might do to us it was just not foreseeing the pivot from televisions to cell phones. We are closer to living the horror of *Videodrome* now with our social media shows than we ever were with television. Anyone can start their own show and become their own character.

    Videodrome is a movie with a lot of retro "cool factor" going for it. It remains interesting to me and saying, "long live the new flesh," never grows old." Depending on how one interprets the film the ending may or may not be satisfying. I assume that it was mostly hallucinations on the part of Max and he is not transcending his old flesh to put on the new, he is merely committing suicide in the end. However, if you think the signal is indeed evolving him and he has a lot more work to do then the ending might be too much of a cliffhanger for you and the lack of sequels disappointing.

Perhaps we will need to adopt a new mantra to fight against the bleak future our devices may steer us toward.

"Kill the algorithm! Long live the old flesh!"

32. NIGHTMARE CINEMA - 2018

Nightmare Cinema is a horror anthology film made up of five short films from five directors. The connecting premise is that different people enter a spooky theater where a man calling himself The Projectionist shows them a horror movie in which they star.

Mickey Rourke is The Projectionist and there isn't much to his character. I think the basic premise of the theater projecting nightmares to people is cool but the creators did not need to hire Mickey Rourke to just look like himself and occasionally say "I am The Projectionist." Rourke added nothing to the movie experience and they dropped the ball on an opportunity to truly craft a horror character akin to say The Cryptkeeper of *Tales from the Crypt* fame. A continuing series of *Nightmare Cinema* films is something that I can easily imagine but not with Mickey Rourke and this version of The Projectionist.

The first short film in *Nightmare Cinema* is known as *The Thing in the Woods* and was directed by the Argentine born Alejandro Brugeus. The main genre feature film of his that I recognize is the 2011 comedy *Juan of the Dead*; though I have never seen it, I have more interest now having experienced the energy of his brand of horror comedy within this short.

"It's not my blood. It's Lizzy's, Maggie's, Tommy's, Carl's, Jamie's, Ron's, Stephanie's…"

The first story launches viewers into the journey of a woman already on the run from a killer, a classic slasher formula scenario, called The Welder due to he wears a welding mask. Poking fun at horror genre tropes is nothing new but the production quality is solid and the flow of jokes kept me amused and tuned in and I was rewarded by the hilarious plot twist. Spoiler: the killer is hunting everyone down because they have space spiders in their skulls piloting them.

At one point the Welder stabs a guy, pinning him to the wall. The victim reaches over to a block of knives to get himself a weapon but the Welder takes that knife away from him and stabs it into him as well. This process repeats itself several times and as horrible as the concept of someone getting a lot of knives stabbed into them is, it was hilarious. The Welder blowtorches the guy from the inside out using a wound to complete the kill—brutal.

The Thing in the Woods has gore and dark humor and I think it set the bar high for the rest of the films when it comes to entertainment value. I will say the actual ending of the short was too expected and generic compared to the fun that led up to it. If one was expecting a scary tone to be set for the nightmares: that does not seem to be the agenda. It is often my experience that anthology films start strong and then just lump some other crap on to fill space. My assumption at the point in the viewing was that things would not get any better.

The second short is known as *Mirari* and was directed by Joe Dante. Joe Dante is famous for having been the director of films such as *Piranha, Gremlins,* and *The Howling*. His addition to *Nightmare Cinema* is well crafted and performed but I have to say that this time the plot twist, while almost as zany as the space spiders of the first story, was also predictable to me.

In *Mirari* a young woman with a scar on her face is sent by her loving man to get plastic surgery in preparation for their wedding. He tells her how it is the same surgeon that his mother, whom the woman has not met, uses to stay as beautiful as she is. It becomes obvious to the woman after the first round of surgery that something is off about her love interest and the doctor who has worked on her and she attempts to escape the hospital. It was obvious to me as a viewer that there was probably going to be a twisted ending involving the mother being freaky looking and the doctors are really carving up the young woman's face to make her also appear freaky. Yep, that was the case. When the face of the young woman is revealed with horrible gashes and her nose sliced off I did find it unsettling even if it was an expected reveal in general.

The third film in this anthology is *Mashit* directed by Ryuhei Kitamura. This Japanese filmmaker directed the 2008 movie *The Midnight Meat Train*. Mashit is the name of a demon and I had a hard time finding it to be an intimidating name because it sounds like someone saying "my shit" in the Southern meets Midwest accents I grew up around. The demon of the title is tormenting the children and adults at a religious school with its special delight being that it makes children commit suicide. The cover art for *Nightmare Cinema* is eye-catching, featuring the demon from this tale; however, I find it is more interesting as a still photo on artwork than how it was presented in the film.

Mashit was dumb to me—a turd. I think the digital special effects are what threw me out of it right away with some badly designed CGI body contortions and broken limbs. I never got interested in the story as it built up to an action sequence with a priest beheading and chopping up possessed children. It really seemed like the shock value of violence against children was the purpose for this tale with the special effects in gore and demon presence looking cheap and silly. The music was also terrible.

The fourth film in Nightmare Cinema is *This Way to Egress* directed by David Slade. Slade directed *Hard Candy, 30 Days of Night,* and *The Twilight Saga: Eclipse.* Slade brought along an actress from the *Twilight* films in the form of Elizabeth Reaser who was Esme Cullen. I actually recognized her from having been in the television series *Grey's Anatomy.*

The definition of "egress" is: the action of going out of or leaving a place. In the short film a woman, Helen, played by Elizabeth Reaser, visits a therapist with her two brat children in tow. The children are not the kindest to her and the receptionist is rude. The receptionist also becomes increasingly odd looking while the entire waiting room environment also becomes caked with dirt and weird. Helen has a short visit with the shrink and then goes about the building looking for her kids who are now missing. She encounters people who appear to be transforming into monsters of some sort. She then sees her children as shadow silhouettes visiting with her doctor behind a door. She overhears them speaking to him about her and it is revealed that she has left her usual plane of existence and they talk about how she needs to kill herself to exit the plane they are all upon. The short ends with her grabbing the entities that have been pretending to be her children and taking them outside into a world that appears dirty or like a sort of ashy apocalypse: the end.

This Way to Egress is cool and makes one think about story possibilities but was not in and of itself a satisfying whole meal of a story.

The fifth film was directed by Mick Garris and is known simply by the title of *Dead*. Mick Garris has played in the horror genre many times directing films such as *Critters 2: The Main Course* and adapting a lot of Stephen King works into moving pictures such as *Sleepwalkers*, *The Stand*, and *Riding the Bullet* amongst others.

In *Dead* a teen boy and his parents are killed by a man but doctors are able to bring the boy back. He returns to the land of the living with the ability to see the deceased and his own mother attempts to lure him to the world of the dead to be with her again. The man who attacked the boy's family arrives at the hospital to try and finish the job as well.

Dead featured a solid jump scare when the man with the gun first appears to attack the family. Aside from that, however, I did not find the story or the acting performances very interesting.

Nightmare Cinema opens with a bang and has some decent moments to experience throughout but I think the opening film is the only one worth seeking out for its fun factor and one would not be faulted for skipping the rest. The later additions to the anthology all seemed to focus on horror involving children, so, if you do not like seeing kids getting hurt then that is another reason to not bother with those portions of the experience.

33. ALIEN - 1979

Many modern movies and television shows are filmed with such dark lighting that my eyes get strained and I cannot tell what is happening on the screen. The 1979 film *Alien* is a movie with a lot of darkness in it but my eyes had no problems during the viewing experience aside from needing to be covered because the events unfolding were too intense. Of course, I am talking about child me of the 80s or 90s, not current me watching the film in 4K. Once I actually got to the age where I could watch scary movies with my eyes wide open, the only scene in *Alien* that I still made sure to glance away from the screen during was the chest bursting scene. The visuals all seem pretty tame to me now but the dark atmosphere and visuals remain rich with intensity after all of these years.

Dan O'Bannon has the screenplay credit for *Alien* but he developed the story alongside Ronald Shusett who has a story by credit on the film. I have heard that other folks altered their screenplay quite a bit, including having introduced the android character of Ash, an element that really steers the story quite a bit, but in all of the shuffling of writers fighting for credits O'Bannon managed to hold on to his creation via sole credit. O'Bannon also has credits on films such as *The Return of the Living Dead*, *Lifeforce*, and *Total Recall*; *Total Recall* is another project worked on by Ronald Shusett as well.

As for the original inspiration for the *Alien* story

Dan O'Bannon has previously made an alien comedy and wished to make a serious film with similar subject matter. The writer is also quoted as having said this regarding where he got his ideas for content: "I didn't steal *Alien* from anybody. I stole it from everybody!" *The Thing from Another World, Forbidden Planet,* and *Planet of the Vampires* are cited influences and when the screenplay for Alien was getting pitched in Hollywood it was being called "*Jaws* in space."

Legendary director Ridley Scott directed *Alien* and it is seen by many as the springboard from which he launched his career into the stratosphere of success. Before *Alien* Scott had only directed the 1977 film *The Duellists*; though he had lots of experience directing in general for television and short projects. After *Alien* Ridley Scott's next feature film was *Blade Runner*.

The crew of a mining spaceship, the Nostromo, respond to a radio signal coming from a planet they are passing by. They check it out to make sure that nobody is in need of rescuing. They find a weird ship crashed on a harsh planet and inside of the ship is a dead giant, humanoid alien creature, but also a lot of egg sacks. A creature, a facehugger, erupts out of one of the eggs and attaches itself to one of the crew. Decisions are made and the afflicted crew member is brought on board the Nostromo with the alien. One thing leads to another and a new type of alien is born and starts hunting and killing the crew of the ship. "In space no one can hear you scream."

They look for the alien, a creature that has become known as a Xenomorph, is based on designs by artist H.R. Giger. It is said that Giger's work was a little too edgy for studio executives but once Ridley Scott saw Giger paintings such as *Necronom IV* he knew that he needed Giger to put his touch on as many design elements as possible.

In the movie the look of the alien is awesome in general concept but sort of weak in execution. There was a man moving around awkwardly in a suit and that was graphic designer Bolaji Badejo. Most of the time when the alien is killing the camera cuts in close or cuts away altogether to limit how silly things might have looked otherwise. I think that the later films in the franchise were able to take advantage of better special effects and Scott and company did a great job of utilizing what they had to work with. For me though on this viewing I say the grimy look of the spaceship and the dark environments are what create the fear factor for the film more so than the look of the alien. However, I guess even if a guy dressed as an alien were popping out of the dark at a person that is pretty freaky.

The facehugger alien is super creepy on screen. I think the filmmakers used some real blood and animal parts when creating the interior of the egg that the facehugger is birthed from and then when the thing perishes and they are looking at its insides. The concept of a weird alien hand thing with a tail latching on to your face and then implanting an alien inside of you that will then burst out of your chest is fairly intense as a concept. However, going back to my early thoughts about the xenomorph not being as intimidating after all of these years to me, I do have to point out that the baby xenomorph that rips out of the man's chest and then skitters away all bloody just adds more fuel to that thought of mine. The alien is funny looking to me, not scary, and this is because the movie *Spaceballs* parodied it and ruined it for me. I laugh every single time I see the *Alien* scene in Spaceballs where the little xenomorph is tap dancing and singing.

The crew saw how the facehugger treated their pal, ala latched on to his face. Therefore, in a later scene when they think it is dead but are not 100% sure it did seem a little odd to me that Ripley and Dallas join Ash in leaning in close to stare at it. They probably should have sealed that thing up safe and sound because they also had seen that it bleeds acid when cut; the acid melted right through several floors of the ship. Yet, there they were staring at it and poking at it again.

As iconic as the Xenomorph is, Sigourney Weaver also made her mark as the character Ripley. She is a tough cookie trying to survive against the alien but she also has realistic emotional breaks that she fights off and I think that it is a star-making performance for sure. She is also sexualized in an odd eye-candy way late in the movie and I think that if the director had gotten his way and the woman ran around naked in those portions it actually would have made more sense than what occurred. Ripley thinks all is safe and she takes off her clothes to get into hypersleep but the tight top and super small panties that she wears make things awkward. The alien is the least of her worries I think because that is one dangerous wedgie she flirts with while showing off as much butt crack as possible. I am not complaining, it just seemed like a weird wardrobe choice. From what I understand, nudity was wanted in the moment to get to a primal vulnerable human vs alien showdown vibe but the studio powers did not want to end up with a porno and nixed the idea. Scott then went with plan B: the tiniest, most uncomfortable panties in the known universe. I have also read that a sex scene between Ripley and Dallas was cut from the production.

For most of the film Ripley is running around fully clothed. I was trying to look up what shoes she was wearing during the film because I think they are a signature part of the character's known "look" but for the most part the Reebok shoes she wore in a later film are what seem to excite people. In this first film she is wearing some Converse shoes.

Dallas is the captain of the ship as portrayed by Tom Skerritt. As I write this Tom Skerritt is not dead but for some reason my brain thought he was. Cast him in a movie, if he is not dead as of your reading of this, because Tom Skerritt to me is an underutilized talent. No Oscar nominations but he did win a Primetime Emmy for the television show *Picket Fences* in 1993.

The character Dallas crawls through the air ducts hunting the *Alien* with a flamethrower. The xenomorph finds him and when it flashes on to the screen it is a solid jump scare sort of moment, yet the way the alien has its arms outstretched made me think if Dallas had just given it the hug it was asking for everything might have turned out better. It is weird that the surviving crew apparently go looking for Dallas after he is attacked and just casually go through the same ducts I guess and retrieve his flamethrower. It is then said that no traces of him were found, no blood or anything, even though the alien tore other people apart in a bloody fashion. So, why did Dallas just vanish? Apparently the alien did not kill him outright nor did it kill the character Lambert, actress Veronica Cartwright, right away, instead using them in some sort of cocoon situation. The scenes with these two characters being used by the alien for breeding or food or whatever it was were cut out of the movie and they are just considered dead in the original release. The scene where Lambert is taken plays well enough that one suspects she was killed but the aftermath of Dallas vanishing without a trace does play odd.

    The entire cast for *Alien* did a great job I think. John Hurt is Kane; he who has his chest burst. Ian Holm is the robot Ash who is really to blame for letting the creature onboard due to the fact that he is following programmed instructions that he and the ship's computer, Mother voiced by Helen Horton, have been given by the corporation in charge. Harry Dean Stanton is Brett and Yaphet Kottot is Parker.

    Ripley's final battle plan in the movie is to self-destruct the main portion of the spaceship while flying away on a smaller ship. The main portion of the ship is apparently equipped with an explosive mechanism that will blow everything up with a ten-minute timer in place. At five minutes the ability to abort the sequence is no longer possible. This leads to a lot of tension for Ripley as she races to not get herself blown up, great for the movie, but I had to pause and think about: why would they have such an unforgiving timer and self-destruct mechanism in place? Seems like such a devastating feature would or should have been designed better with a programmable timer or unlimited time to abort.

    After Ripley defeats the xenomorph, knocking its butt out into space where it then tries to climb back into the ship via a rocket booster and gets blasted away, the final shot of the film with her peaceful in her sleep chamber, paired with the music, is quite the lovely end to such a dark adventure.

Alien is a classic for a reason and is still a strong film regardless of time and pop culture references having attempted to water down the memorable scares and moments overall. I would say that in this viewing I gained a new appreciation for the performance of Sigourney Weaver as Ripley.

34. DISTURBIA - 2007

After seeing *Disturbia* for the first time back in 2007 I thought it was entertaining. Then I heard through the entertainment news grapevine that the movie was sued for being a ripoff of the film *Rear Window*. I was under the impression that the creators lost the suit and forked over a bunch of money. As it turns out the movie was sued, not for being similar to *Rear Window*, but for being similar to the short story *It Had to Be Murder* upon which *Rear Window* was based. The lawsuit was actually thrown out though another was filed. I do not think *Disturbia* ended up being legally too similar to the other property as I had been led to believe. The film is a fix of thriller, horror, and teen romance that is actually quite the feat for the production team to have pulled off in a commercial sense.

Shia LaBeouf stars as Kale, a young man put on house arrest due to having punched his teacher. Kale is prone to acting out because his father died in a car accident that he blames himself for. While on house arrest Kale spies on his neighbors and develops a crush on the new girl next door Ashley. Sarah Roemer portrays Ashley. A less appealing neighbor is Mr. Turner portrayed by David Morse. Kale, Ashley, and Kale's buddy Ronnie begin to suspect that Mr. Turner is a serial killer and they work to try and expose him for his crimes. Carrie-Anne Moss is on the cast as Kale's mother Julie, Matt Craven is the father who died in the opening, Jose Pablo Cantillo is Officer Gutierrez who makes Kale a special project of his to harass, and Kale is also monitored by Detective Parker portrayed by Viola Davis.

Christopher Landon and Carl Ellsworth share the

screenplay credit for *Disturbia*. Landon has gone on to direct genre films such as *Happy Death Day* and *Freaky*. Ellsworth wrote on the Wes Craven film *Red Eye* and the remake of the Wes Craven film *The Last House on the Left*. Nothing to do with these guys or *Disturbia* but I wrote a screenplay called *Breath of Hate* that as a movie got its titled changed to *The Last House* and whichever brain at the distributor who made that decision now has that movie buried in search engine obscurity under all of *The Last House on the Left* material. Hey, I am not successful enough and have not made enough movies yet not to whine and complain every chance I get about the circumstances around the few that I have.

    D.J. Caruso directed *Disturbia* and he teamed up with Shia LaBeouf again soon after for the action thriller *Eagle Eye*. An earlier film directed by Caruso that I have always found interesting is *The Salton Sea* starring Val Kilmer.

    Disturbia blends different genre elements together and it is a slick production. It might test the patience of many people when it comes to how adults refuse to believe Kale when he swears his friend has been taken and such but I guess grownups are that uncaring sometimes from a teenage point of view.

    The opening scene of tragedy is a burst of violent car crash action that ends with a shot of Kale looking into the wreckage at his father. What he sees is left to the imagination of the audience but the camera position and the look on LaBeouf's face sell it as something horrible indeed.

    The romance between Kale and Ashley might not sit well with more modern audiences because basically she falls for her peeping Tom. There is a scene where she confronts him about how often he watches her from his house and he gives her all the details he has observed and why they make him like her. She says his words are either the creepiest or most romantic things that she has ever heard. And then she kisses him. In real life I think most people would vote creepy, so, any peeping Tom's out there who think this type of behavior is going to sweep any women off their feet: think again. In fact, the scene that sets up this smooch between the characters is Kale having a fit that she is socializing with other people, jealous she might like another boy, and he does what he can to try and ruin her night and control her in some way.

When the killer decides he has had enough of the snoopy kids and sets about trying to kill them, the movie gets intense enough I suppose. There is a cool stunt where Kale and Ashley escape his house out of an upstairs window, leap to a garage, and then go off that into her swimming pool next door. I guess I am writing this paragraph just to reiterate what *Disturbia* does right: it entertains. Grab the popcorn, I'd watch it again.

35. PET SEMATARY: BLOODLINES - 2023

Pet Sematary: Bloodlines, how do I hate thee? Let me count the ways. I'm just kidding. NOT. "Not" was kind of big in the 90s but would probably make some of the newer generations of folks cringe and think: "Were people really that dumb back then?" Or "Man, 90s fads sure were dumb." And with *Pet Sematary: Bloodlines* ruder me wants to think either the people making it were dumb or they think that audiences are dumb; either way I guess I sound like a jerk and I hated the movie. Bringing up the 90s has nothing to do with nothing to this point either but dang some movies inspire me to lack cohesion and not make much sense.

Lindsey Anderson Beer directed this lackluster affair and she also wrote it alongside Jeff Buhler. Now that I have named the captain of the ship I feel bad about trashing the movie in my opening paragraph. Maybe things went wrong in the filming process and the good stuff wasn't able to make it into the movie for some reason or another; I don't know. This movie has watchable production value for sure. It is not as bad as, for example, those Humpty Dumpty killing people movies I have seen. I think I wrote about one of those flicks in the first volume of *Horror Movies Binge*. Ugh. Now that I think about that Humpty Dumpty crap I feel better about *Pet Sematary: Bloodlines*; apologies. I'm still going to make fun of it though.

When capturing performances for a movie one

wants to be drawn in by the performances and forget that it is a movie; this is how you will scare me or make me cry or wouldn't it be great if a horror movie scared me and made me cry at the same time? But, then, like, you know, made me happy after that. The entire cast of *Pet Sematary: Bloodlines* does a solid job but they just seem like actors acting, not people living in the skin of the characters. I bet in an audition room or in an acting class I would think them quite skilled, but for some reason their strengths did not play on screen as compelling, if that makes any sense.

    I like the casting for this film, someone did a good job in that department overall. I am not saying the performances were all that great but I enjoyed seeing some recognizable older actors alongside some youngsters I did not recognize. It was cool to see Henry Thomas, David Duchovny, Pam Grier, and Samantha Mathis hanging out. While Duchovny and Thomas got the most screen time I think the most amusing moment came from Pam Grier when her character Marjorie Washburn is shown after a scene where it looked like she might have been killed by a mean dog. She shows up with some wounds on her face later and it is a fun turn of event to hear that she bested the creature.

    Jackson White portrays the leading man of the film as Judson. He fits the part and the era I felt regarding basic look. However, this leading character is a bit dull. It felt like a side part character who would have been gutted and forgotten about, fodder for the body count in a slasher. I am not blaming anyone for my lack of connection to his journey though, it was okay stuff in general I guess. There are some scenes where the actor is holding a hunting rifle all tight to his shoulder as he goes into a house ready to shoot a killer and save his girlfriend and it looks like he or he and the director were making sure he held the gun properly. It looked silly to me though because it wasn't like he was in an open field and going to shoot something at a long-range distance. In the tighter interior of that house, he would have a hard time holding the gun like that and being able to raise it up in time to aim and shoot and all of that. I guess I am saying I felt like I was watching an actor trying too hard to look like they knew proper gun handling techniques.

Natalie Alyn Lind portrays Norma the blond lady love of Judson. She didn't draw me in either but she does some solid running for her life barefoot and then appears to have been a gamer getting bound up and all muddy in a hole. Norma's escape from that hole was weak though. She is bound and trapped in a muddy hole that is slowly filling with water. Judson is trying to find her and save her and there is an attempt at tension showing that he may not make it in time. And: he never does. Norma kicks some mud, as she had been doing, and finally some of the Earth gives away and I guess somehow that means she was magically able to untie herself and escape the hole? Huh? She just shows up, running to greet Judson.

Forrest Goodluck is the character Manny. I found him okay and likable enough I guess.

Jack Mulhern plays Timmy Baterman, who is a dead soldier who got buried and brought back to life. I think he did a good job of posing around as a creepy fellow. Isabella LaBlanc also plays someone who is brought back to life: Donna. I think the actress did an okay job but she just was not creepy, Donna was not as creepy in comparison to Timmy. The undead were not very scary to me in this at all.

Speaking about the undead, the story never explains what is going on very well. I am familiar with the rules of the *Pet Sematary* stories, starting with the original tale as told by Stephen King. However, if you have not seen the other movies or read the book then chances are that from the opening frame of this flick you will not understand what is going on.

The year is 1969 and Fox Mulder, err, Bill Baterman, is dragging a dead body for some reason. Then there is a creepy dog at some point and a draft dodger looking for his place in the world outside of his town discovers a horrible curse that is in his town.

The dog bites Norma and she goes and spends some time in a hospital bed recovering. Dog bites are a bit scary and I have been bitten several times in my life. One time a dog got me pretty good on the wrist and the wound kept hurting and bleeding so I went to the hospital. They told me it looked like it could use a stitch but that they don't stitch animal bites, gotta let them breathe. So, away I went breathing out of my wrist until the hospital bill showed up and I died. NOT.

Judson and Manny realize there is something wrong with their friend Timmy. They discuss it and decide that the best way to figure out what might be making Timmy act weird is to go to the church where they keep the old town records. WTF. Your friend acts weird and so you go look at old town records? Where is the connection made there? Then on top of that nonsense there is a drunk priest and he is like, "Hey kids, guess what, I just happened to find these extra spooky old records hidden in a piano, check them out." WTF. OMG.

FTBAMTS. That last one is "flipping the bird at my television screen." Sorry. The 90s guy is trying to seem like he is "with it." NOT.

Dan Crandall is an expert on how to handle people brought back by the bad magic of the pet sematary. He tells the kids that they have to shoot the undead in the eyes to stop them. A few moments later he busts into a room to save the day and shoots undead Donna with a shotgun. He did not shoot her in the eyes. Then he turns his back on her and acts like she is down for the count. Sir, you said to shoot them in the eyes. Donna pops up behind him, stabs him, kills him—what an idiot. It would have been fun if he was supposed to be an idiot and the shooting them in the eyes thing was just him not knowing what he was talking about and the kids end up realizing that after shooting out some eyes and not defeating the monsters or something. Eye wounds are shown though, so, I guess shoot them in the eyes.

Mr. Baterman has seen the error of his ways and is helping the rest of the cast track down his son to destroy him. It doesn't go so well; one thing leads to another and their plan to burn down the house kicks off with the fire starting while they are still inside of the house. Baterman though has a plan: "This place is on fire. We've got to get out of here. We can wait it out in the cellar!" WTF. You don't wait out a fire in the cellar. You would burn or suffocate or have the burning house above collapse onto you. I am not even sure how David Duchovny found it reasonable for his character to say those lines.

Pet Sematary: Bloodlines is a frustrating experience that I wouldn't recommend anyone else watch so that the evil is stopped. Well, unless a person just wants to watch it so that they can whine about it like me. Or to whine at me: "Yo, 90s dude, your whining was not rad at all."

36. THE WOMAN IN BLACK - 2012

The Woman in Black is a British film that was directed by James Watkins. He also directed *Eden Lake* which I watched in my first *Horror Movies Binge* book. The screenplay credit is held by Jane Goldman who also has credits on big movies such as *Kick-Ass* and *Stardust*. I knew that Harry Potter starred in a ghost movie but I never got around to seeing it until now!

Daniel Radcliffe is Arthur Kipps who is still bereaved from having lost his wife when she gave birth to their son. In order to provide for his son, he must take on a job for a law firm that sends him to a small village where a woman has died leaving behind her creepy old mansion. Arthur is tasked with sorting through the woman's old papers. However, once in the house he starts seeing the ghostly sight of a woman wearing black and every time he sees her a child in the village dies. Ciaran Hinds plays Sam Daily, a key helper to Arthur in solving the mystery around why the woman is haunting the area. Janet McTeer portrays Sam's wife.

The location is the most interesting thing about the movie in my opinion. The creepy old mansion is on an island with the only road to it being one that disappears with the tide. They get some amazing shots of the road and water. In reality this setup does not exist and the island is actually Osea Island which has a population on it not living in a single creepy mansion. The exterior shots of the mansion in the film are Cotterstock Hall in central

England.

The townsfolk that live in the village near the island know about the woman and black and wish for Arthur to go away. However, no one outright explains their fears to him and some kids have to die before he starts figuring out things for himself and with the aid of Sam. Arthur is shown to have some belief in ghosts and such and I just felt like the town folks instead of just being randomly crabby toward him as an outsider should have been more upfront with him because it is the lives of their children on the line. Furthermore, it seems like some of them might have considered moving far away from the area for the sake of their kids.

If you do not like seeing kids die then *The Woman in Black* is a sinister tale indeed. Three girls hop out of a window together in the opening, there is a muddy drowned boy running around with pale ghost children, a girl drinks some lye and vomits out blood before she dies, and then one girl sets herself on fire. The girl who sets herself on fire was locked in a room by her parents to protect her from being killed like their previous child which did not actually make any logical sense to me. The ghost makes children commit suicide if anyone sees her.

There are some creepy toys in the film and the camera really enjoys cutting to them often. It began to affect the pace and one clown toy specifically got its face shown time and time again as filler.

Even though the movie does drag in some parts I thought the acting was good and the overall story was a "cute" ghost story from start to finish. Arthur discovers a ghost that wishes to be reunited with her dead child and he sets about doing this in order to save the children of the village and his own child en route to visit him. It seems like he succeeds but the angry ghost is not the forgiving type I guess and she makes Arthur's son step out onto some railroad tracks in the finale. Arthur jumps down to save his kid and for a moment you are left wondering if maybe they made it. They did not. Father holds son and the boy turns and asks, "Who is that woman?" Arthus says "That is your mommy." I mean, he really says it like "mummy." And then you see the ghost wife reunited with her family and the ghost family walks away happily ever after. I guess the woman in black DID return the favor in a twisted sort of way: she got her dead son brought to her and she reunited a dead woman with her son and husband.

 The final shots with the happy ghost family were a little too much in my opinion. I like the ending well enough regarding the tragedy that occurs but I would have ended it on the father and son looking off in the direction that they do and Arthur informing the boy that the woman they see is his mother, without actually showing the mother.

 The Woman in Black is a solid tale with some cool visuals regarding the setting. I did not find it all that scary though, but I could see it getting closer to the nerves of those who do not venture into horror all that often and came to see what Harry Potter has been up to.

37. EVENT HORIZON - 1997

Event Horizon is a 1997 horror film that some have dubbed *The Shining* in space or *The Shining* meets *Alien* meets *Hellraiser*. It was directed by Paul W.S. Anderson and writing credit went to Philip Eisner. I have read that the script originally had tentacled aliens from another dimension attacking people but those were taken out because the director did not want to make an *Alien* knockoff and wished to make more of a haunted house in space experience. The screenwriter is said to have admitted that he ended up making the spaceship that warps into a Hell dimension story because of his familiarity with the game *Warhammer 40,000*. I have never played *Warhammer 40,000* but I guess there are spaceships that warp to some place and come back spookified. Some fans of *Warhammer* lore consider *Event Horizon* a prequel movie for the game.

    The Event Horizon is a spaceship that disappeared while exploring the unknown edges of the universe. The ship utilized a special warp drive designed by a man named Weir. Seven years after disappearing the ship returns and a rescue crew is sent to investigate along with Weir. Once the rescuers are on the ship they start seeing scary visions and the ship seems alive and intent on scaring them by giving them perverted visions based on their own fears.

    There are a lot of jump scares layered into the sound effects early on in this film, doors slamming and such, and I think that a new viewer gets the hint right away that this film means to "get you." Once I was old enough not to be covering my eyes and plugging my ears during a horror film I never really found any moments in them to be "scary." However, I can recall teenage me being asked by someone once what the scariest movies were and I think I said that there were moments in both *In the Mouth of Madness* and *Event Horizon* that were scary-ish. Both films star Sam Neill, he is Weir in this film. As big of a fan *Jurassic Park* that I was, also starring Sam Neill, I bet my attraction to the two horror films I mentioned was due to them not being as popular or well known, giving me something to pull out of my trivia hat to interested parties that didn't watch as many movies as I did.

    The most memorable moment of *Event Horizon*, the scary part, is just a couple of seconds of footage flashed on the screen. The newcomers find footage from the original crew and glimpse the torture and horror they were enduing, complete with glimpses of a bloody orgy with mangled participants and one fellow reciting Latin while holding his own eyeballs in his hands. It is said that the gore and violence of this film got toned down and a lot of footage lost due to studio edits and interference. An extended version of the "found footage" moment of this movie if found by some unsuspecting person could be quite intense if they popped it into the ole VCR I bet. It is said that the scene took a lot of effort to shoot with porn stars and amputees brought in to really let the imagination of the creators go to some twisted places with flexibility. I have read that the crew felt very dirty afterward.

    The spaceship in this movie is designed with

horror in mind for sure with one hallway looking as a character describes it "like a meat grinder." It might have been cool to see the ship during happier times so that when it is haunted one would have a comparison to make regarding how darkly things really changed.

    The timeline in the film is laid out as such:
    2015 – First permanent colony established on the moon.
    2032 – Commercial mining begins on Mars.
    2040 – The Event Horizon disappears.
    2047 – Present Time.

    Paul W.S. Anderson shot this movie after having directed the 1995 video game to film adaptation of *Mortal Kombat*. He made two gritty films in a row with *Event Horizon* and then the action film *Soldier* but the video game turned film series for *Resident Evil* is probably the franchise that he is most known for and they have more CGI slick than grit in my opinion.

    Event Horizon was pushing the special effects limits with its production and I can recall the blend of anti-gravity sights with horror in space at the time marveled quite a few. The effects do look dated now but I think the dark tone of the film compensates for the goofier looking effects and keeps them from ruining the experience. Or maybe I am more forgiving because I was a fan of the film when I was a teen. Either way I think this film is a property ripe for being remade with modern technology.

    Lawrence Fishburne is the character Miller who is the captain for the doomed rescue mission and the main hero for the final fight sequence of the film. Fishburne is strong in the role but the character sacrifices himself to save two of the other surviving crew members and this makes my mind crave more regarding the fate of Miller. He transports with the ship presumably into the hellish world that the previous crew went into and I have a morbid curiosity as to what suffering or transformations he may endure. Miller seemed much stronger in constitution than Weir. If they ever get around to making a reboot or a sequel I would hope to see Miller return in some form.

As for the fight against Weir and the ship in the ending moments, well, that does not play out all that interesting. Weir blinds himself and has his face a mess of gory wounds but is defeated in a lame manner at first by him simply being an idiot and shooting out a window which in turn leads to him getting sucked out into space. So, the possessed ship and the entities it steers or creates might be freaky but not bright. But then Weir magically returns to face Miller in a final battle scenario and I have read this was done only because studio executives did not think that Miller verses a burnt demon of a memory from his past would play as well for audiences. It does make some genre sense to prop Weir up longer as a key villain, ala something a potential franchise can hang its hat upon, ala a Jason, Freddy, or Michael Meyers but I think having him sucked out into space and then returning was not the best storytelling decision overall.

Kathleen Quinlan, Joely Richardson, Jake Noseworthy, Richard T. Jones, and Sean Pertwee are all actors who helped fill out the rest of the crew in the movie. They were all compelling in their own ways. I do not think that the visions of Quinlan's character Peters made much sense regarding helping me buy into the ship, really tricking the crew with such things. She keeps seeing her child wounded and running around the ship and she knows it can't be true, yet she keeps being fooled into thinking he is really there. I cannot get my own mind around the logic in her mind at falling for that when she seems quite mentally capable of discerning that she is seeing things that are not really there. Really that goes for the entire crew—they know a game is afoot yet they still sort of fall into it as players/victims.

Jason Isaacs is the other crew member, D.J., whom I found the most interesting. He is the medical officer but I can sense that there is some interesting material in his backstory not fully explored within the confines of what is the *Event Horizon* story. There is a darkness in the man of some sort and I would have been interested in learning more about him; there is something creepy or dangerous about him I think. He does end up getting quite the twisted death, hung up in the medical department with his chest spread wide open.

Another super creepy character, perhaps the creepiest, is Claire, portrayed by Holley Chant. Claire appears in visions to Weir as his wife who appears to have slashed her own wrists in a tub. The paleness of Chant's flesh paired with the idea of a razor opening it, the blood flowing out, really is an artistic vision of horror pulled off successfully.

"I have such wonderful things to show you."

Yeah, with that above line the filmmakers weren't even trying to hide that they appreciated the vibe put forth by Clive Barker's 1987 *Hellraiser* film.

Event Horizon remains a solid watch but the flaws

stack up and make the story teeter more for me these days. I see it as a great candidate for a reboot with the action pieces needing to be better thought out with logic and execution and the ending being made more satisfying in some way.

38. AMERICAN PSYCHO - 2000

American Psycho is a psychological satire horror film that follows a serial killer as he shares his psychotic world view as a greedy Wall Street fellow in the 1980s. The man begins to lose his grip on his cold mentality and questions his own way of life, his bloodlust spirals into a frenzy that leads him toward seeking accountability for his actions, to come clean to everyone about the secret life he lives.. When he confesses no one cares. The meaning in this journey is a heck of a thinker and *American Psycho* remains a unique experience all of these years later.

  This film was released to theaters in the same year that I graduated high school. I lived in "the sticks" and my buddy and I would sometimes drive forty-five miles to Jefferson City, Missouri to watch movies. Late late movie showings were not an uncommon adventure and I can recall us buying tickets to an *American Psycho* viewing of that nature and the dark ride home featured two young men more confused than energized by the film that they had seen. The film had challenged what we had assumed it to be and even though I did not fully grasp the meaning behind it all I leaned toward having enjoyed the film more than not and knew that I would need to watch it again.

  This film is based off a novel by Bret Easton Ellis. Other films based off this author's work include *Less Than Zero*, *The Rules of Attraction*, and *The Informers*. I am a fan of *The Rules of Attraction* and after all these years it is after my latest viewing of *American Psycho* that I realize that the one of the leading characters from that film, Sean Bateman, is Patrick Bateman's younger brother. Aside from being a mass consumer of movies I have always been an avid reader but the fact is I have never read a Bret Easton Ellis book; shrug emojii. The book *American Psycho* was published in 1991.

 Mary Harron wrote the screenplay along with Guinevere Turner. Harron also directed the film and Turner acts in it as the character Elizabeth, a friend who is a friend of the lead killer character Bateman who gets talked into a threesome and then doesn't seem to make it back out from under the covers alive.

 Mary Harron is said to have come close to working with Billy Crudup as her lead actor but after he left the project she ended up getting Christian Bale to read the script and she zeroed in on him as Patrick Bateman. It was not an easy task getting the movie off the ground with Bale in the lead because it is said that the movie studio wanted Leonardo DiCaprio to star. Harron was removed from the project and Oliver Stone came in and started tweaking things with DiCaprio set to be the lead. However, it is said that Stone and DiCaprio did not see eye to eye in a creative sense and both left the project paving the way for Harron to return with her continued insistence that Christian Bale be cast as Patrick Bateman. Ewan McGregor is said to have been offered the role but the vision of Harron and Bale obviously won out.

 Christian Bale is an actor known for living the parts that he takes on and Patrick Bateman was no different. Perhaps the authorities should open up some of the cold case murder files from the late 90s and see where

Bale was on the nights in question. Okay, mainly he probably studied some psychos and then did physical transformations, in this case getting super buff with exercise, using a lot of face cream, developing an American accent, and getting dental work done. Author Bret Easton Ellis is said to have been creeped out by the actor having first met him at a lunch in which Bale arrived in character instead of as himself. Christian Bale brought to life a horror character that may not have been franchise material in a Jason, Freddy, or Michael sort of way but iconic, nonetheless.

Jared Leto portrays Paul Allen and gets killed by Patrick Bateman with an axe. The scene features Bateman critiquing the band Huey Lewis and the News while they listen to the song *Hip to be Square* from the musical act. The scene is perhaps the most memorable and has been parodied by singer Huey Lewis himself taking on the Bateman role and killing Weird Al with the ax. When a movie scene becomes iconic and parodied, sometimes the parodies can ruin the original scene after subsequent viewing over many years. *American Psycho* is special to me in that it defends itself with its strong satire being impenetrable in that regard, that scene remains as fun and interesting to me as it ever was. The monologues that Bateman launches into, reciting critical thoughts about popular pop musical acts to seem more human and relatable, are always amusing.

Jared Leto, Chloe Sevigny, Reese Witherspoon, and Willem Dafoe are all actors whom I always recall having been featured in *American Psycho*. However, on this viewing I found myself going, "Oh yeah, there's Josh Lucas and Justin Theroux." Cara Seymour, Samantha

Mathis, Matt Ross, and Bill Sage also get their screen time.

Cara Seymour is the prostitute who makes the mistake of hanging out with Bateman twice, with the second time perhaps being one of the second most memorable moments from the film. After a threesome turned bloody, Cara's character Christie runs from Bateman who is naked in sneakers and toting a chainsaw. He watches her flee down a flight of stairs and then drops the chainsaw with perfect timing to hit her as she reaches the final steps.

I have read that director May Harron has heard complaints over the years about Patrick Bateman being homophobic. She has pointed out that such a complaint is an odd one to focus on when they are talking about someone who is murdering people. Like, that is the bad trait that turned them off about the film? Patrick Bateman is a psycho, not a hero, and in the scene where he goes to strangle Luis, portrayed by Matt Ross, in a restroom is possibly one of the offending "homophobic scenes." It is hilarious though. Luis turns as Bateman puts his gloved hands to his throat and instead of seeing the act for what it is, thinks that Bateman is coming on to him sexually. He lets Bateman know that he has been longing for him for a long time and is happy that he has finally made a move. The killer reels away in disgust and rushes to the sink where he washes his hands. The detail that had me grinning is that he is still wearing the gloves that he put on as he washes his hands.

The moment that made me laugh aloud though happens during Patrick Bateman's final rampage of violence. He is confronted by a woman as he tries to feed a cat to an ATM machine and he shoots the woman. This catches the attention of the police and after a car exploding shootout, Bateman runs into a building where he shoots the security guard. As he runs from this murder into a revolving door he realizes that a janitor has stepped out with a mop and bucket. The sight of Patrick Bateman going full circle through the doors back into the building to shoot the janitor before resuming the exit through the doors is what made me laugh.

It also cracks me up that Patrick Bateman keeps on saying "I have to return some videotapes," or tells people he was returning videotapes.

"There are no more barriers to cross. All I have in common with the uncontrollable and the insane, the vicious and the evil, all the mayhem I have caused and utter indifference toward it I have now surpassed. My pain is constant and sharp and I do not hope for a better world for anyone. In fact, I want my pain to be inflicted on others. I want no one to escape. But even after admitting this, there is no catharsis; my punishment continues to elude me and I gain jo deeper knowledge of myself. No new knowledge can be extracted from my telling. This confession has meant nothing."

American Psycho is a classic.

39. THE EXORCIST: BELIEVER - 2023

The Exorcist: Believer was directed by David Gordon Green who has an interesting directorial body of work. He made a name for himself with dramatic Indie films such as *All The Real Girls*, *Undertow*, and *Snow Angels* and while he has continued to explore drama with projects such as *Prince Avalanche*, *Joe*, and *Stronger* he also transitioned into being an in-demand comedy director with films such as *Pineapple Express* and *Your Highness*. The horror genre has become another hat worn by this filmmaker with a *Halloween* trilogy under his belt: *Halloween*, *Halloween Kills*, and *Halloween Ends*. I watched the first of those three efforts and it did not inspire me to pay attention to the sequels. They must have been good enough to impress someone though because David Gordon Green was able to secure a deal to continue the *Exorcist* series with another trilogy; from what I understand the ink stated that three films would get made regardless of how well the first one, *Believer*, turned out.

David Gordon Green wrote the screenplay for *Believer* along with Peter Sattler with Scott Teems and Danny McBride also getting story credits. It looks like there were a lot of cooks in the kitchen but the end result to me felt like a lot of bare bones with little meat on them.

The opening of the film is an elaborate setup for a woman dying while giving birth to her child. The woman, Sorenne, portrayed by Tracey Graves, is in Haiti with her photographer husband Victor who is portrayed by Leslie

Odom Jr. After a busy day of hanging out in some markets and then getting her baby blessed in some voodoo ritual Sorenne gets to suffer injured in a major earthquake. Victor is given the classic choice of saving his child or saving his wife and years later he is hanging out as a single parent with a daughter. Lidya Jewett is the daughter Angela Fielding and with the amount of backstory given to her character it sort of seemed weird to me that the other lead girl Katherine, portrayed by Olivia O'Neill, became less important, sort of setup to be thrown away it seemed like, like—two girls are possessed but who cares about Katherine?

   The lack of content for Katherine and with her parents being portrayed more like jerks than Victor does not completely make one not care about her character's fate. The fact that she is young and suffering goes a long way toward developing some empathy I think and her tragic end still plays as a dark note of emotion regarding visuals. However, it could have been deeper and darker and instead of shying away from developing her as well as Angela one could have torn out our hearts like the demon was tearing out her soul. THAT would have made this a memorable horror movie!

   Maybe I should not have skipped to talking about the ending so soon? Anyway, Angela grows up and is friends with Katherine and the two girls go hang out in a creepy hole/tunnel place in the woods and try to contact the spirit of Angela's dead mother. It was a confusing scenario overall and the manner in which the girl's become possessed ends up being lame in my opinion. The girls vanish for a few days, then turn up, and then they start acting all spooky. The casting department managed to get two kids with large foreheads and maybe this sounds mean but once they applied all of the horror makeup to the girls they began to look like Chucky dolls from the *Child's Play* series to me.

I am not making fun of the girls, even looking like haunted dolls or something I thought that both of them did a great job twisting around and having fun with their roles. I would not call it scary though.

Katherine's father was actor Norbert Leo Butz who I recognized from the Netflix show *Bloodline* as Kevin Rayburn; I only saw the first season of that series. Katherine's mother was an interesting casting choice to me and I liked her screen presence while I tried to put a finger on why I recognized her. Jennifer Nettles is Miranda and she is not a face that I associate with acting, rather she is known to me as the singer for the country band Sugarland.

Ann Dowd is the character Ann Brooks and I thought that she was compelling in the role as an irritated neighbor who is then a nurse to the girls at the hospital and then takes the lead on orchestrating an exorcism.

As a direct sequel to the first *Exorcist* movie this film manages to give fans a fun scene with the return of known characters. Ellen Burstyn is present as Chris MacNeil who was the mother from the first film. She delivers some bland monologues and gets her eyes jabbed out in the movie. Her acting was some of the weakest in the film really and I have read quotes from her that suggests she did not care about being there and only cared about the money. However, Linda Blair is brought into a scene as Regan MacNeil, the possessed girl from *The Exorcist*, and that is indeed a cool moment just for the sake of fandom and pop culture fun.

One point of the story was to show common ground within the framework of different religions. People with different religious views come together to try and free the two girls of the demon within them. In this attempt to show how different religions actually have core beliefs that are fundamentally the same, I was reminded of that old Saturday morning cartoon *Captain Planet*: "By your powers combined, I am Captain Planet!" Or in this case, Religion Kumbaya! They did sort of give the Catholic fellow the "hero" moment of deciding to do the right thing, he's joining the circle of folks played like it meant the most. He gets his head twisted around for his effort shortly thereafter; crunch.

The other main aspect of the story is sort of a Biblical moral fable akin to that story where the king is trying to figure out who is really the mother of a baby and threatens to cut the baby in half. In this case the demon offers the parents the choice of saving one of the girls while damning the other; Deja vu for Victor to some degree, right? Katherine's father is weak, breaks, and declares that his daughter should be the one spared. The demon fakes out that it is killing Angela but it is all a trick and it kills Katherine and Angela is the blessed survivor.

The last time that you see Katherine she is in a hellish, water filled hall of sorts being drug down by scary monster people arms. Yikes. Poor kid. It is a creepy shot and ending but as I mentioned earlier I think the power was stolen from it by Katherine's journey not getting as deeply developed as Angela's.

The Exorcist: Believer was very watchable in my opinion; it surprised me that I did not have trouble sitting through it. However, it is also one of those movies that afterward I found way more to nitpick at than to praise and in looking at Internet review scores for the film I understand why more people than not seem to rate it low. There were cute ideas but not all cute ideas make for stunning cinema and the parts did not align making it all goofy not scary.

40. SNOWBEAST - 1977

There are childhood memories of a yeti creature stalking skiers drifting around in my head. Every now and then the images of white fur and snow pops the question: "what movie was that?" It wasn't a mystery that I felt pressed to solve but solve it I did, the 1977 made-for-television movie *Snowbeast* made an impression on youngster me. Now it is time for oldster me to give it a gander.

Herb Wallerstein was born in 1925 and died in 1985. In that life he found the time to direct a lot of episodes for television shows such as *The Farmer's Daughter, Star Trek,* and *Gunsmoke*. He directed *Snowbeast* based off a screenplay by Joseph Stefano. Mr. Stefano was born in 1922 and died in 2006 and his most notable movie writing credit is for the 1960 film *Psycho*. Most critics figure that the duo were trying to capitalize on the horror success that was the 1975 film *Jaws*. So, Jaws but with a bigfoot instead of a shark and far more boring.

Apparently all it took was some roaring and a furry arm to impress me as a movie watching little kid. *Snowbeast* features some POV camera work of the creature coming at people with very few glances at the actual beast costume itself. Mostly though the runtime is filled with footage of people skiing very slowly around in the snow. They do switch things up and feature some extended snowmobile driving footage but more silly creature feature costume shenanigans would have been better.

There is a beast seen on the mountain but old Carrie Rill can't let her boy Tony Rill scare off the guests for the annual Winter Carnival or whatever. Sylvia Sidney is Carrie Rill and Robert Logan is Tony. Tony thinks about hunting the beast on the down-low for a bit but eventually the creature decides to go public on its own, attacking a gym full of people enjoying the carnival. Sheriff Paraday joins Tony on the hunt for the beast and he is portrayed by Clint Walker. There is an attempt at developing an odd love triangle with a gold medalist skier named Gar Seberg arriving at the resort with his wife Ellen. Gar needs a job because he has lost the respect of his wife by being a bum and refusing to ski again after winning his medals all those years ago. His drama about being scared to ski again because he is afraid he can never top how good he skied on that medal winning day is as silly as the fact that he goes to a ski resort looking for a job. Tony has the hots for Ellen, who at one point had the hots for him before she chose to marry Gar and just as it looks like she and Tony might rekindle those feelings right under Gar's nose, Gar straps on some skis and crunches around in the snow like a real man. Bo Svenson portrays Gar and Yvette Mimieux is Ellen.

"It's not an animal but not human either."

The above quote was a weird thing to say I thought but really most of the dialog is nonsense aside from that. The acting performances are fun though, classic movie style efforts where the performers do their darndest to sell the drama regardless of how ridiculous it is.

I guess the best lines come when Tony is brought in to identify the body of a woman that has been mauled; a random guest that he may or may not have crossed paths with at the busy resort.

"Maybe I'll recognize her when I see her face."

"She doesn't have one."

This moment in the movie reminded me of my cousin Clinton and how anytime when we were young and it came to scary story time he would go with: "There once was a boy who had no eyes and no nose!" Ahh! Yeah, cousin Clinton wasn't giving anyone the jeebies.

When Tony tells Gar about the snowbeast, Gar is offended for the creature that Tony wants to kill it. It is weird how insulted he gets but then he comes around to being the one to kill it in the end. Gar and Ellen are both very accepting of there being such a thing as a bigfoot or Yeti monster which is amusing. Ellen is a reporter and she has heard about such things before and tries to sort of be the expert on their existence.

I need to let my memories of *Snowbeast* melt away. I could be using that brain space for better knowledge I bet. I guess it is not that easy though and I am cursed to know that *Snowbeast* exists.

41. LISA FRANKENSTEIN - 2024

Lisa Frankenstein is the feature film directorial debut of Zelda Williams. Zelda indeed got her name from the princess in the Zelda video game series as bestowed upon her by her famous father, the late Robin Williams. Visually I think the movie packed in the fun as a blend of 80s comedy meets goth Tim Burton-ish flair and with cool tunes to boot. However, I do not think an original or rich "atmosphere" was created in an artistic sense that is going to make me remember this film for years to come. It will be interesting to see if Zelda Williams carves out a unique voice for herself though as a director.

The screenwriter for the film was Diablo Cody who I believe may have gotten the ball rolling on the project as a producer as well. Movies working with Cody scripts tend to have a specific style of dialog and in batches it can come across sometimes as trying too hard to be hip and quirky. I am not hating on the style, I think there are a lot of fun gems to experience in the lines the characters deliver. Diablo Cody won the Best Screenplay Oscar for the film *Juno* and isn't a stranger to the horror genre either, having been the writer for *Jennifer's Body*.

Diablo Cody is a stage name with Cody having been born Brooke Maurio. If you are not familiar with her Hollywood fame story it is an interesting one. As a writer she was trying out different blog ideas but seemed to have found a popular niche writing about her life after quitting her day job to become a stripper. If I understand the timeline correctly her blog led to her getting a memoir book deal and then someone suggested she also write screenplays and badda-bing a Hollywood success story is born. I do not know the truth or actual details and a lot of Hollywood stories play with facts behind mirrors while smoke is blowing out of someone's butthole, somewhere in there Cody was writing for a newspaper and Entertainment Weekly I think too, BUT it does make for an inspiring tale if you are someone who doesn't believe you go from the stage of a strip club to the Oscars ceremony in a lifetime. Life can be stranger than fiction, get to writing!

    The plot of this film centers around a teen girl, Lisa, who, after her mother was killed by an ax murderer, lives with her dad, stepmom, and stepsister. She is an outsider with no friends at school and enjoys spending time next to the grave of a young man that died in olden times. Aside from a lack of friends Lisa's stepmother is not nice to her at all, she has a crush on a guy that she is too timid to really talk to, and at a recent party another guy took advantage of her with some sexual groping. Lightning brings the dead guy out of his grave and Lisa is inspired by him to change her attitude and to go after the things she wants in life. The undead fellow gets protective of Lisa and when her stepmother threatens to send her away he knocks her over the head with a sewing machine. This fatal blow is the first murder that Lisa and her new undead pal orchestrate as he seeks to replace his rotten body parts with fresh ones. They kill a person, lop off the desired piece of anatomy, Lisa sews it on, and then she zaps the rotting fellow in a malfunctioning tanning bed to make the parts functional. Yes, the groper loses his hand.

The killing shenanigans escalate to a point of no return and Lisa senses that she is doomed. Also, I guess that love blossoms between her and the dead guy.

Lisa Frankenstien stars Kathryn Newton as a teen named Lisa Swallows. I recognize this actress from the horror comedy *Freaky* in which her character experiences a body swap with a serial killer. It is interesting to see that she starred in a role poking fun at that popular movie plot trope and then also takes part in a movie that lightly features the teen plot trope of an outsider getting a makeover of sorts to turn heads at school. Kathryn Newton does a fine job in the lead in this film but the movie is more style than depth so it is an entertaining comedy skit style of performance more than not.

Cole Sprouse plays The Creature. He is known by many as one of the lead child actors in the Nickelodeon show *The Suite Life of Zack & Cody*. He was Cody. He also starred as Jughead on *Riverdale* and he was the kiddo from the Adam Sandler movie *Big Daddy*. In this film he mainly lurches around and makes noises but he has solid screen presence.

Lisa Soberano is the stepsister character of Taffy and I thought that this was possibly the best character in the movie. She is the popular girl and sometimes says things that one might expect from a "mean girl" type but she is not mean at all. She is super supportive and loving toward Lisa and always trying to get her to come out of her shell. It is a fun play on what could have been a cookie-cutter sort of role, a twist away from the expected formula.

Carla Gugino portrays the evil stepmother and I found this character to be more over-the-top obnoxious than the rest. However, it is a silly movie to begin with. As for the father of Lisa, that is Joe Chrest as Dale. If you have seen this actor in a show or movie before he has a lane and he sticks to it in his performance for this flick. His act of being an oblivious parent is amusing.

As I watched *Lisa Frankenstien* and saw how quickly Lisa was to embrace murder I assumed that maybe she is the one who actually murdered her mother in the past, not some crazed ax murderer. This is never revealed to be the case so her journey does feel a little odd and hollow.

I think that the word "hollow" is a good description for this film. There are funny bits and it is an enjoyable watch but I did not find any characters to truly care about. Lisa flips into joke cracking psycho a little too easy and the love story with The Creature did not get strong development either. Lisa makes a decision in the end based on love but I don't think the romance really got to that point between the two—the sparks might have been flying in the mad scientist tanning bed but Cupid's arrows were not obvious to me. Of course, she is a teen, and falling in and out of love can be a fast roller coaster ride I suppose. I think the movie *Warm Bodies* did a better job of crafting a romance between a living girl and an undead fellow.

The content of the movie tiptoes on that PG-13 line with splashes of blood and even a gag involving a penis getting severed off of one boy and glued onto another. *Lisa Frankenstein* is an amusing film that I think should have gone for an R rating to pack in more punch.

42. TERRIFIER 2 - 2022

The first *Terrifier* movie was my introduction to the character of Art the Clown. I think that the contents of the movie made me feel a little icky at times but I could appreciate the dark humor and the performance of David Howard Thornton as the killer clown. Now to put the character to the test with the sequel: is Art the clown a phony or an icon? Can the filmmaker harness the goodness in the evil to make a time worthy franchise?

Terrifier 2 was written and directed by Damien Leone and even with the production of the film getting interrupted by the Covid pandemic shutdown he kept working at developing the material and it paid off in the form of a successful theatrical run for the film. I have read that because of its low budget *Terrifier 2* was one of the most profitable films at theaters in 2022. I bet many people were curious and introduced to Art the clown for the first time because of this sequel.

The goal seems to have been: bigger and better with this sequel. Damien Leone fleshed out a heroine sort of character to battle Art this time which changes the vibe of the series in some ways. They stay true to the original formula with the violence and gore but there is an attempt at making characters that you care more about. I even found myself rooting for the meat to get away this time, not just wondering what Art's next horrific gag would be.

A young woman named Sienna and her brother become the targets of a resurrected Art the Clown. Art also has a spooky little girl clown that hangs with him as well. Sienna's father was an artist that got a brain tumor and then killed himself in a car crash. Somehow he knew about Art the clown and drew pictures of not only him but of his own daughter as an angel warrior. He also left her a sword and Sienna appears to have intense dreams related to Art that may have some sort of meaning. A lot of new worms were sprung out of the can for this over two hours long sequel.

    Lauren LaVera is the leading lady for *Terrifier 2*. She brings a strength to the series with her acting chops and makes for a compelling hero to follow. I guess the character going around as a warrior angel is something Leone has been obsessed with for a while and it is neat to see someone manage to get their battle angel vs clown movie made.

    Sienna's little brother Jonathan is also a main player in the story. Elliott Fullam portrays this character and he is okay but his performance was also one of the most annoying elements of the film at the same time. Any time the kid is trying to show that he is scared the facial expressions and blinks are just terrible. Kudos to him though for taking on so much work in a film where a clown keeps violently abusing him; Art flails him and even bites into him a few times. It seems like children getting hurt has been a theme in the movies I ended up watching in this binge.

    Sarah Voigt is Barbara, the mother of Sienna and Jonathan. I found her gruff performance amusing because of how often she cusses at her kids. Barbara ends up getting her face blown off by a gun and then Art sets her up at the dinner table and makes her some mashed potatoes. Jonathan gets to watch the clown slap mashed potatoes into the gory hole where his mom's face used to be. As messed up as that sounds I think it was also the last kill in the film where I felt the playfulness and dark humor landed. All the kills after that did not vibe exactly the same in their brutality.

    The Little Pale Girl is what the little girl clown is called in the credits of the movie. I sensed she might have been a former victim of Art's but the full details and why he can see her and she is participating in some of his madness is lost on me. In an early scene it is shown that the girl is only visible to Art, however, Sienna and Jonathan can see her at the end of the movie. Amelie McLain portrayed this character and she does a good job posing around in creepy makeup; another child actor taking part in a vicious movie, when she is first introduced it appears that she releases a stream of diarrhea into the floor and things just get worse and wacky from there. Visually this character was a danger regarding stealing the show away from Art along with the vision Sienna makes for her Halloween angel costume.

    "Dude, you should have been here, a couple of birds were eating his asshole."

    There is a scene where some kids find a dead opossum behind a dumpster at their school. A teacher interrupts them and it is actress Felissa Rose. Felissa Rose first made her mark on the horror genre as Angela in the 1983 film *Sleepaway Camp*. She also happens to have been in the movie *Silent Night Zombie Night* that I produced and played a realtor in the movie *The Last House* that I wrote. She may or may not remember who I am but she seemed nice in all of my interactions with her. In *Terrifier 2* her cameo is literally just a single brief moment and line and I wish that she had gotten to face off against Art.

Tamara Glynn is another horror actress with a cameo in the film: Costume Shop Mom. Glynn is known from the 1989 slasher *Halloween 5: The Revenge* of Michael Myers as the character Samantha Thomas. Her *Terrifier 2* scene merely has her bringing her kid to the Halloween store but they find that the place is closed. The kid peers through the glass and can see Art the Clown inside holding the severed head of the cashier. The kid thinks that it is a cool prop. The joke of children seeing Art with a severed head is used twice in the film. Later he serves candy to some trick or treaters out of the skull of a decapitated woman.

Another cameo in the film arrives in the credits. The wrestler Chris Jericho portrays an orderly at the insane asylum where the disfigured Victoria Heyes resides. Victoria is the survivor from the first film that then attacked a reporter interviewing her. Actress Samantha Scaffidi portrays Victoria and judging by the final sequence it seems she has some strong magical connection to Art akin to The Little Pale Girl. Art was beheaded by Sienna with The Little Pale Girl collecting the head and walking off with it. But then Victoria gives birth to Art's head, it is alive, in her cell to set up his return for a third flick.

Art the clown still managed to crack me up in this film. The funniest bit for me that made me laugh is when he is trying on sunglasses in the Halloween store harassing Sienna. At some point though the humor faded and Art quit being funny. Maybe this is due to the movie being too long or the kills not being as high impact after the brutal bedroom torture scene. I don't know, his gags were not as creative, his violence remains brutal but instead of being amused by any of his quirks I was too busy hoping for him to be defeated.

    The bedroom scene in which Art brutally mutilates Sienna's friend Allie is probably the one that most people will walk away from *Terrifier 2* scarred by. I laughed aloud when Art tried on sunglasses but as he butchers Allie I spoke these words aloud: "That's awful." At one point Allie is disfigured, missing an arm, and crawling across her bedroom floor and Art brings in some bleach to douse her with and some salt to rub into her wounds. This is a prime example of how his clown antics set him apart from the average slasher villain, the kill is horrible, actress Casey Hartnett's screams have you feeling for her, but the dark humor layered on top is something special. "That's awful. Oh my God it is also kind of funny."

    Another friend character in *Terrifier 2* is Brooke portrayed by Kailey Hyman. The acting really helps this film take a step up from the previous installment and I think that Hyman did a great job as well with her part. Of course, she is rewarded by having acid thrown in her character's face before she is smashed open and Art pulls out her heart for a snack. And that happens to her after she witnesses Art stab her boyfriend in the crotch a bunch and then play around with his severed penis. I feel like with Brooke that maybe having her spike Sienna's drink with drugs in a previous scene might have been an attempt to make her less sympathetic of a victim but it did not work. As she tried to get away from Art I wished her to survive.

    A missed opportunity in the scenes with Art

chasing Brooke I think is the bag of coke that was in the car. There could have been some gag involving a clown snorting coke to bring in a chuckle. At this point in the movie, I was out of chuckles.

When I was younger I would often go to late movie showings at the theater and as I watched *Terrifier 2* I imagined that seeing such a thing on the big screen after midnight would have been an interesting experience. There is a lot of entertaining production value in the movie with retro vibes woven in tight via the soundtrack and overall, I got a distinct *A Nightmare on Elm Street* vibe also; not the first film but some of the sequels, probably *A Nightmare on Elm Street 3: Dream Warriors*.

Terrifier 2 expands on the lore of the first film with many magical elements that were never fully explained. There are mysteries left open and that is frustrating. I think the hero vs villain journey played out as a standalone experience but all the unanswered questions still left the movie feeling incomplete. There is a franchise here with Art the clown for sure but I prefer a movie to be a movie and not feel purposefully episodic with story elements brought up not explained. Why did their dad know about Art the clown? What are the origins of the clown? Why is the sword magical? How is Sienna magical? What is up with The Little Pale Girl? All these elements are brought into play but without better explanations I have more frustration than curiosity with the storytelling. I'll check out *Terrifier 3* when it comes out and for anyone who cannot stand extreme gore, I agree this sounds like a morbid choice to make but Damien Leone is on to something, there is still a lot of potential for the series, and I want to see where he goes with it.

43. THE MIST - 2007

The Mist was written and directed by Frank Darabont based off the 1980 novella by Stephen King. I did not grow up a Stephen King fan, preferred Dean Koontz but I have grown to appreciate King more as an adult just because it can be hard to find stuff to read and I always know that I can pick up one of his books and it'll be a smooth enough experience. Frank Darabont must be a big King fan though because he directed two other adaptations of his work prior to this one: *The Shawshank Redemption* and *The Green Mile*. After *The Mist* Frank Darabont created the television show *The Walking Dead* and one can see some of the same actors, not on the Tom Hanks level, who appeared in his films made it into his zombie show as well.

After a thunderstorm a mysterious mist sweeps over a town and people are quick to realize that there are dangerous things in the mist. The story follows a large group that takes shelter inside of a grocery store. Thomas Jane is the main lead Dravid Drayton but there is quite the ensemble putting in the work with some of the actors being: Toby Jones, Laurie Holden, Andre Braughner, Jeffrey DeMunn, William Sadler, Frances Sternhagen, Sam Witwer, David Jensen, Melissa McBride, Alexa Davalos, and Chris Owen.

Marcia Gay Harden is also on the cast as Mrs. Carmody and I have separated her from the main list because it is that type of performance. She is scary in *The*

Mist and just because she won an Oscar for the 2001 movie *Pollock* doesn't mean Mrs. Carmody wasn't the better performance or award worthy as well; she did win a Saturn Award for it. Mrs. Carmody goes from being considered the town kook to being a leader within the store preaching her version of the Bible and reality. Her ability to gain followers and the way she lashes out at those who do not join her flock make her one of the most memorable villains ever. It can be quite frustrating to watch her sometimes but that is a good thing, she gets under the skin.

    I watched the trailer for *The Mist* before this latest viewing of the film and the special effects in the trailer were really bad looking. I recall them not being the sharpest back when the film was released either, therefore, I assumed I was going to see some goofy looking creatures attacking the people in the grocery store. It was a pleasant surprise, however, that the tentacles and bugs and such did not look that bad really; when the store worker Norm is drug out by some tentacles was probably the weakest looking CGI. I watched the 4K version in color but there is a black and white version and I bet the movie is taken to another level in that visual flavor.

    The aforementioned character Norm was portrayed by Chris Owen. If you grew up with the movie *American Pie* perhaps you know the actor better as The Sherminator.

    The mist in the movie is said to have leaked into our world from another dimension. Scientists at a military base are blamed in the film. I do not think they needed to give a reason or origin for the mist for the story to work and would have preferred such a detail to have been worked around without explanation.

There are some horrible deaths in this movie but the earliest one that checked off the boxes of being tragic and grotesque would be Sally. Sally is a young woman who works at the grocery store and she seemed very kind. She gets stung by a giant bug that breaks into the store and the horrid way that her face bloats up as she painfully dies is disturbing.

This movie is one of the most depressing movies ever. David, his young son, and three other adults get into his vehicle and attempt to drive away from the mist. They run out of gas and are still trapped with all the killer creatures. The group decides that it would be better to kill themselves rather than get eaten by mutant spiders or alien creatures. David kills them but does not have a bullet for himself. As he steps out of the vehicle hoping to be eaten, distraught with grief after having just killed his own kid, soldiers arrive and it appears as though they have a handle on the situation now. The group was only moments away from being rescued. Total bummer.

There was a woman portrayed by Melissa McBride who left the grocery store early on in the movie to get back to her children. She pleaded with the others to go with her and help her but no one would. She was forced to go out into the mist alone and presumed dead. The morbid cherry on top of the distressing ending is that as David wails out as a broken man this woman is shown in one of the passing vehicles as someone that survived and was rescued by the soldiers.

The Mist is scary because of the people in it and the way they act in groups when dealing with fear. It is a study that is as relevant today as it was the year the film came out. People get swept up in causes and chaos and I think that watching this movie could perchance deprogram some people from negative behaviors; probably a slim chance, my faith in humanity was not strengthened by the film at all. This movie works like a mirror of reminder that we need to strive to be better. *The Mist* will forever be a relevant comment on human nature and is an important film.

44. BURNT OFFERINGS - 1976

Once I had the guts to add horror movies to my stacks of VHS rentals as a child I discovered the 1976 film *Burnt Offerings*. I became fascinated by the ending of the movie and would rent it and sit through it just to once again see the character Ben Rolf fly out of that window and smash head-first through the windshield of his car. It is a scene that has never left my mind but the title of the movie is one that I always forget and every few years feel the need to do some internet sleuthing to figure it out. Now that I have found it again and am writing about it perhaps I won't forget again. However, I must say that the title is a tad confusing to me. I get the offerings part but nothing gets "burnt."

Dan Curtis directed *Burnt Offerings* and wrote the screenplay along with William F. Nolan. The screenplay is based off the 1973 book written by Robert Marasco. The story follows a family who lands a great deal on a vacation home but once there they find themselves being affected by the house. Essentially they are offerings to the mansion and it feeds off people to rejuvenate its walls and bring back the owner of the house: "mother."

Oliver Reed stars as the father character Ben Rolf. The man becomes mentally anguished while inside the house with recurring nightmares about a grinning chauffeur driver that was at his mother's funeral. Anthony James portrays The Chauffeur and his smile just proves that even the simplest of things can be made creepy.

Ben also becomes violent toward his son David. Lee Montgomery portrays David and the scene in which his father attempts to drown him in the pool is somewhat intense in my opinion. Fathers can be scary and if you have ever had an ill interaction with yours seeing Ben go from playfully tossing his kid around in the pool to trying to drown him might trigger you.

Is this movie actually scary? No. I do not mean to mislead you in that regard. *Burnt Offerings* is a ridiculous soap opera with whack-a-doodle dialog and all the actors have dialed up their theatrical drama skills to an eleven on a ten-point scale.

"But I don't want a goblet! I want a glass!"

There are moments one can set aside and find creepiness in, true. Overall though I would describe *Burnt Offerings* not as scary but more awkward or a movie that is in a perpetual state of dramatic weirdness.

"I don't forget things. I know what I do!"

Legendary film star Bette Davis is the elderly Aunt Elizabeth on vacation with the family. She is turned against the child David as well and, at one point, sneaks into his room and turns on the gas to try and kill him in his sleep. David surviving the gas "leak" occurs after his dad attempts to drown him and one would think that instead of contemplating leaving the house so much that the family would have high-tailed it out of there.

Aunt Elizabeth ends up in a weird state of possession on her bed and Bette Davis does a grand job of looking disturbed as she groans and twists on the bed. She dies in that scene, probably of natural causes, but visually the grinning Chauffeur bursts into the room and slams a coffin against the bed.

Karen Black stars as the mother character Marian Rolf. She becomes obsessed with cleaning the house and taking care of it. When they move into the place they are told that the elderly owner of the place resides in the attic and Marian is to take her meals each day. It is shown that Marian eats the meals and in the end she becomes the vessel that "mother" takes over as the new mother of the house.

Actors Eileen Heckart and Burgess Meredith are the people who rent the house out to the family in the beginning and Dub Taylor is the handyman also featured in those scenes.

If one is seeking to find meaning in the story of *Burnt Offerings* it is a popular opinion to say that it is a statement against materialism. There is also a lot of dialogue and jabs at how people are perceived in old age with the old lady being referenced upstairs, Aunt Elizabeth, being touchy about people considering her to be old, and then the old house seeking to be restored to its former glory.

For me *Burnt Offerings* is all about the ending. The Rolf family are finally making their escape but Marian decides she must go back inside one last time to tell the old lady upstairs goodbye. When Marian does not return, Ben goes in after her leaving David alone in the family station wagon. Ben discovers that his wife is upstairs sitting in a chair and has transformed into the old lady of the house. Marian gives him a gruff look and the next thing we see is Ben comes flying out of the upstairs window. The man plummets down and lands on the car with his face penetrating the windshield. The look of his dead face in the glass paired with the blood splattering onto David are morbid images of cinematic gold.

David gets out of the car and he doesn't get to escape either. The chimney on the house breaks apart and the stones tumble down crushing the boy. The end.

Burnt Offerings is ridiculous but it is a sort of awesome ridiculousness and in a few more years if I have not been thrown out of any windows I might seek it out to watch it again.

45. THE HUNGER - 1983

The Hunger is a vampire film—though no one ever calls anyone a vampire technically—from 1983 that I somehow skipped watching until now. There is a chance I saw it when I was young and forgot it but no bells were ringing during the viewing regarding scene recognition. It is a moody film with a lot of interesting threads woven into the story details.

Tony Scott directed this film and it is considered his feature length film debut. I am a fan of Scott's work but this trivia fact is new to me. Heck, I didn't even know he directed it until I started watching it and his name was listed in the credits. *True Romance* is probably my favorite Tony Scott film but the man had a unique way about him when it came to action films in general, a vision that stood out as he went farther into his career with flashy films such as *Man on Fire*, *Domino*, and *Deja Vu*. In the end he seemed fairly obsessed with trains and finished his career with the train films *The Taking of Pelham 123* and *Unstoppable*. *Unstoppable* is a movie that surprised me with how exciting it was because I went into it lacking Scott's enthusiasm for trains but it's a thrill ride indeed.

Visually *The Hunger* is a very dark film and I see a lot of people regurgitating that the film was not an immediate hit but found a cult following with people into "goth" style and trends. It is easy enough to see the appeal in that regard, I mean, the movie does literally open up with the musical act Bauhaus, considered goth rock pioneers, singing *Bela Lugosi's Dead*. The movie is a bit on the "artsy" side regarding how it is cut together and telling the story. I found that aspect interesting enough but I can understand if someone were not in the mood for the style and wished to accuse it of being more like music video directing at times. But, hey, I got my teenage brain addled by music videos on MTV and then Michael Bay came along and changed the pace of action films to a great degree too. *The Hunger* is not as frantic as, say, Tony Scott's action fever dream that is *Domino* but you can see him testing out some things, taking some style chances for sure.

    One of the coolest shots to me is simply some corpses in trash bags being thrown into an incinerator early on in the film. It is morbid but the open mouth of one of the victims outlined against the taunt plastic as the flames begin licking at them is a creative sort of haunting that I won't forget soon.

    One might think that as a guy I would be itching to type about the ladies in the movie smooching all over each other's bodies but I actually found the most interesting aspect of the movie to be David Bowie's character John. The sexual aspects of the film did not overpower the tone set by his depressing fears over aging, dying, and being put to the side by the woman he devoted his life to. When I think of David Bowie and acting I generally think of him as Jareth in *Labyrinth* but he puts in a memorable performance in *The Hunger*.

    The screenplay for *The Hunger* was written by James Costigan and Michael Thomas based off the Whitley Streiber novel published in 1981. It follows a female vampire named Miriam and her companion John.

It seems as though Miriam has been around for thousands of years, perhaps with Egyptian origins of some sort and John has been with her for hundreds of years but he starts to rapidly age and discovers that the eternal life promised to him was a lie. Miriam seeks to replace him with a new lover in the form of Sarah Roberts who just so happens to be a doctor studying the process of aging.

The most fascinating aspect of the story to me is how John ages suddenly but dying is not his actual fate. He withers up into an old shell of a man that Miriam then carries upstairs and places into a coffin alongside her other former lovers. A great premise to base a horror story around! However, the second half of the movie is more about Sarah being seduced and transformed and I actually was wanting to see John teaming up with the aging doctor to try and salvage his existence as the main plot.

Susan Sarandon portrays Sarah and when she is curled up in bed, sweaty in a shirt and socks, fighting off the hunger for blood, well, if you are into vampires this is where the sexy is at. I mean, Sarah and Miriam do get naked on the bed and lick at each other in an earlier scene but I don't know, I think for a change of pace the fighting against the vampire urges is more erotic here. Sarah ends up stabbing herself in the throat in a suicide bid to stop herself from becoming Miriam's newest slave.

Miriam is portrayed by Catherine Deneuve. I think that all the actors did a fabulous job in *The Hunger* but will admit that with her French accent I did not understand portions of what Deneuve was saying.

When Sarah stops the process of her transformation by stabbing herself in the throat I did get confused. This action makes the crusty corpses gain the energy to attack Miriam and then she herself deteriorates away into death. The final shots of the movie show Sarah having survived her wound and I assume she is now living as Miriam was with her powers transferred over to her. Miriam is trapped in a coffin crying out. It is interesting but confusing and I have read that the studio forced this ending to set up sequels that never happened. I have read quotes from Susan Sarandon also being confused about her character's fate being altered.

  There is a kid in the film named Alice, portrayed by Beth Ehlers, who is a musical student of Miriam and John. Her presence keeps the movie binge streak alive of kids being harmed in horror movies that I apparently have going. The elderly looking John needs to feed but he might also be worried that Alice will one day be his replacement and he ends up killing the child. For this kill to happen though he needed to let Alice in the house and she was visiting just to tell Miriam that she would not be making it to her next rehearsal. It felt odd and forced to me how the kid insisted she be let inside to write Miriam a note. I also think it could have been interesting to see John feeling even more pathetic, perhaps while bathed in the blood over this kill.

  Some of the close shots and slow-motion stuff in the film kind of made the action bits bland. One sequence involving a visit to the attic featured a lot of birds fluttering around and the sounds of them fluttering really started to get on my nerves.

  A notable cameo that caught my eye in the movie occurs when Sarah is making a call using a phone booth. Two fellows hang out near the booth and one of them is actor Willem Dafoe.

The Hunger is interesting regarding some of the elements it brought to the table but it felt like there could have been some deeper exploration. So, aspects of the story grabbed my attention but the overall tale of the movie did not go anywhere fulfilling to me. There have been rumors of a remake over the years and I can easily see this as another property that could have some flaws nipped and tucked to jazz it up. Yes, Hollywood is too quick to remake things, but in some cases I feel like it is akin to when a new band covers an older song, sometimes the cover is cool too, and I see *The Hunger* as a movie with potential in that way. Of course, I did not grow up with it or help it reach its supposed goth status so apologies if I offend anyone who loves it in its original format. I never was "goth" but I did once buy a pair of pants from a Hot Topic that had chains dangling off them!

46. NIGHT OF THE LIVING DEAD - 1968

In 1968 George A. Romero cemented himself into history as one of the forefathers of horror films due to his work with the living dead, the undead, or dare we say: zombies? In *Night of the Living Dead* no one calls the ghouls zombies but it has become popular for the sake of pop culture simplicity to refer to the types of killers featured in the film as such; even if it also means this gives some other argumentative person a lane to gripe about how the definition of a zombie shouldn't include blah, blah, blah. It has been a long time since I have sat through *Night of the Living Dead* and this showing was the OG black and white version.

Aside from directing *Night of the Living Dead*, George A. Romero also co-wrote the screenplay along with John A. Russo. However, I have read some quotes from the actors implying that there wasn't much of a script and we can give them credit for large chunks of what ended up in the film. The story contents of the film center around a small group of people who take shelter inside a farmhouse when dead folks start wandering about killing the living.

Zombie films over the decades have brought us all sorts of variations of the entities but when thinking of *Night of the Living Dead* I remembered the film featuring classic, slow, stumbling corpses that are mostly a threat when in larger groups. The movement speed for the zombies varies in the film with the first dead guy ambling along at a quick pace at times. The living dead in this film also use tools which seems to imply that they are not one hundred percent moronic. They use rocks to break windows and make clubs for themselves to bash things. Some of them also react as if in pain when struck; I saw zombies throw up their hands to cover their struck faces more than once. There aren't any truly vile looking corpses shuffling along in the film, most just look like regular ole disheveled folks not having a great night. One is naked. *Night of the Living Dead Streakers* might make for a fun movie.

  As I watched the zombies I wondered about the dead still inside their graves. Were they digging their way out? Were they animated too? I reckon they needed to still contain brains in their skull, therefore, I guess rotted corpses with decayed brains would not have come to life. The way I understood it the zombies had their brains reanimated when a satellite that picked up mysterious radiation from Venus exploded on its return to Earth. The radiation is what brought the dead back to life.

  The living dead wish to eat other humans. I am not sure what drives them to dine on flesh because sometimes they only bite people and those people join the zombie ranks. Also, they are shown eating some people they have just died in an explosion, mmm BBQ, but they do not attack one another. Yeah, the logic is a little screwy.

  I mentioned that the zombies in *Night of the Living Dead* are more dangerous in groups than not. Well, the same can be said about humans that are alive. When people get together in large groups they get into some evil hive mind shenanigans. *Night of the Living Dead* could have been titled *Night of the Idiots* in reference to the humans trying to survive.

Duane Jones portrayed the character Ben who is more or less the central hero. He takes charge by sealing up the house and protecting Barbra who is so shocked by what is going on that she spends the rest of the movie between being a comatose idiot or a babbling idiot. Barbra was portrayed by Judith O'Dea. It turns out that there are more folks hiding in the basement of the house and when they make themselves known to Ben and Barbra the man Harry Cooper argues with Ben about the best course of action to ensure survival. Harry is portrayed by Karl Hardman. The rest of the Cooper family consists of Marilyn Eastman as Helen and their daughter Karen portrayed by Kyra Schon. It is the face of Karen that one often sees in artwork for *Night of the Living Dead*; the kid that was bitten by a zombie and then later turns, taking a bite out of dad and killing mom.

There is another couple taking shelter in the house as well. Judy and Tom are a couple portrayed by Judith Ridley and Keith Wayne.

Harry wants the group to stay in the basement and Ben wants them to remain upstairs. The men argue and the narrative really slants things toward showing Harry to be less heroic than Ben. It is true that Ben cannot trust Harry and eventually they get into a scuffle over the only gun and Ben shoots Harry. Harry stumbles down into the basement—one of the worst man dying routines ever performed—and his daughter that has turned into a zombie does take a bite out of him. Harry turns into a zombie too and when Ben goes downstairs he finishes the execution with the gun.

The kicker about all the fighting between Harry and Ben and the perception of Ben being a hero and

Harry a whiner is: as the potential sole survivor Ben ends up having to take shelter in the basement just like Harry wanted the entire time. Ha ha.

"They're coming to get you, Barbra."

The opening scene in the graveyard where Barbra's brother Johnny annoys her is fairly amusing. They get attacked by a monster and while Johnny wrestles with it Barbra runs away. Russell Streiner portrays Johnny and when it comes time for the annoying Barbra to meet her end, not only does a group of "they" pull her out of the house but Johnny turned zombie himself leads the effort.

When Barbra carries around a knife inside of the house for a weapon she is sometimes holding it by the blade. Ouch.

The scenes when it is only Barbra and Ben in the house are some of the most boring to have to sit through. Ben tells a long story about how he witnessed zombies chasing a truck and it sounds like the movie George A. Romero might have made if there had been the budget for bigger stunts. If you have ever wondered what someone means when they say to "show not tell" regarding something in a script or film, well, watching Ben TELL about the zombie action is boring but if the director had been able to film the actual scenes and SHOW the action it would have been far more entertaining. It doesn't help that right after Ben gets done telling the story Barbra launches into a story about her and Johnny that we actually DID see happen already. Yeah, seeing something and then also having to sit through a verbal recap of it had me squirming in my seat.

Tom and Judy are the couple killed in the explosion. Tom and Ben are going outside to pull the truck around to a gas pump with the intention of fueling the vehicle so that everyone can then jump in and the group can drive off. Judy goes full idiot and decides to run outside to join the group as they embark on their mission. Tom is an idiot that has never pumped gas before I guess because he squirts gasoline all over the place. Then he bumbles around and lights the gas on fire. Tom and Judy drive off in the flaming truck that then explodes.

      Helen Cooper is killed by her daughter in the basement and when the living dead crash into the house Ben finishes off the zombie family downstairs and awaits to be rescued. The rescue party arrives, Ben goes upstairs, and they mistake him for a zombie and shoot him dead. Yeah, *Night of the Living Idiots* gave way to *Day of the Living Idiots*.

      The final shots of the film are still photos of what happens to Ben's dead body. Men stand around him with big hooks in several shots and then they use the hooks to lift the corpse for transporting to the burn pile. Ben is an African American man and seeing him surrounded by those hooks made me think about the 1992 film *Candyman* based off a Clive Barker story. The story that *Candyman* is based off of is *The Forbidden* and in the original story it sounds like he is a Caucasian killer with a hook for a hand. However, the film version stars a not Caucasian Tony Todd. It is probably a coincidence and my brain is connecting dots with imagery association and Candyman's film design was not influenced by the imagery of Ben and hooks. However, to add more fun to this line of thinking is that in the 1990 remake of *Night of the Living Dead* the role of Ben is played by Tony Todd.

Night of the Living Dead is a little dull with a lot of filler talk and news reports. However, it is easy enough to understand how it shocked audiences upon its release and the ending of the film is still as strong a kick in the gut as it ever was to witness. Those dumb zombies really got me thinking about how dumb people tend to be. I can see connections between the tale told in *Night of the Living Dead* and the movie *The Mist*. I prefer *The Mist*.

47. MANIAC COP - 1988

Maniac Cop is a battle between large chins: Robert Z'Dar vs Bruce Campbell. Here is the thing, I knew Robert Z'Dar was in the movie but I did not know his name but I did not know that Bruce Campbell was in the movie while I do know his name. Robert Z'Dar's big chin, by the way, was the result of a medical condition: cherubism. The appearance of people with cherubism is caused by a loss of bone in the mandible which the body replaces with excessive amounts of fibrous tissue.

The plot of the movie is simple: a giant, maniac cop is on the streets of New York killing people. Robert Z'Dar is the killer cop. I assume he is undead or that there is something supernatural in play because they shoot him and it does not hurt him. He is a cop who got sent to prison and was either murdered there and came back to life or survived when everyone assumed him to be dead. I did not really catch the facts regarding why he seemed indestructible. The cop is out for revenge against those that sent him to prison but he just kind of murders at random too.

Bruce Campbell is not really the first lead of the movie. It seemed like Tom Atkins as the detective Frank McCrae was the leading guy. He gets thrown out of a window though and dies before the final showdown. I found his character amusing out of the gate because he just right away is all onboard with the killer is a cop. Some thugs chased a lady and when she ran to the maniac cop for help he killed her. The police capture the thugs and do not believe their story about a killer cop, except Frank, he just knows there is a killer cop, no investigation needed.

Laurene Landon is the character Theresa. Theresa is the mistress of Bruce Campbell's character Jack. They are both police officers. Theresa is more of the hero in this movie in my opinion; out to get things done. Jack kind of bumbles along, gets captured, and is not truly hero material in general. He is mistaken for the maniac cop and he and Theresa are trying to clear his name. Jack is not really a guy the storyteller ever makes you want to root for, because when you first meet him it is in an argument with his wife and then he leaves to go have sex with his mistress at a motel.

Laurene Landon looks to have worked with the writer of *Maniac Cop* quite a few times. She actually set out to become a policewoman before changing her mind and pursuing acting.

William Lustig directed the movie. Lustig has directed two sequels to *Maniac Cop*, which I have not seen, and lots of other flicks. I have seen his 1996 slasher *Uncle Sam*. It looks to me like *Maniac Cop* is destined to be his mark that he made or his Hollywood legacy.

Larrey Cohen wrote the screenplay for *Maniac Cop*. He has 88 writing credits and not all of them are B movies. The films *Phone Booth* and *Cellular* both have his name on them. I wonder what the story is with him writing back-to-back thrillers involving phones? Cohen also has 21 directing credits including the 1974 flick *It's Alive*.

Maniac Cop is a slasher movie but it has an 80s B

action movie spirit going for it. There is also a cool stunt in the end where the maniac cop drives a police truck into the river with Jack holding on to the side of it. Jack backflips off the side of the truck as it goes airborne and flips in the other direction.

At times the humor of the film made it feel like it was being steered toward *Police Academy* territory. There is a scene where Frank's boss complains that he never smiles and the forced smile that actor Tom Atkins delivers does give the scene an end to chuckle at. I actually think the movie would have ended up being more entertaining with the character of Frank surviving until the end to fight the maniac.

This movie had me giving it a shot and going with its vibe all the way until the ending where it lands with a wet splat. Jack is trying to stop the maniac but all he is really doing is holding on to the side of a truck as it is driven away. The maniac—Matt Cordell is the character name—pretty much defeats himself. He drives straight into a large metal pipe that impales him and then he crashes into the river. It is a dumb ending. Of course, when they pull the truck out of the water he is not in it and it shows him under the pier seemingly having survived. I guess no one will spot him and that explains how there are sequels.

The lack of a solid ending or exciting final showdown is what killed *Maniac Cop* for me. There is a little struggle and a car chase but really the hero characters were not at all that interesting and pair that with the dumb end sequence and I am disappointed that I spent the time that I did watching the movie.

48. NIGHT SWIM - 2024

When I was a kid I can recall taking swimming lessons where they tied milk jugs to our arms and threw us in. I was terrified and did not learn to swim from those lessons. Heck, after a few splashes with jugs I went to the shallow end stairs and clutched onto them for dear life. I remember they brought my mother in to try and bribe me off the stairs into deeper water. She offered to buy me a candy bar if I would participate better in the class but I did not fall for it. I taught myself how to swim when I was a teen by just getting into a pool and waving my arms and legs around like other swimmers. I am not afraid of swimming pools; the ocean is intimidating though and there are some creepy things lurking about in lakes.

Night Swim is not a movie that was on my radar and when I read that it was about a haunted swimming pool I figured I was in for a shiny studio turd of a horror experience. Things get wet but as it turns out *Night Swim* is not a wet turd. Consider me splashed with positive surprise.

Bryce McGuire wrote the screenplay along with Rod Blackhurst. McGuire directed the movie which is an expansion of a short film that the duo created. Short films tend to be a waste of time in my opinion but I can see their usefulness if trying to use the material as a proof of concept piece or to show off one's talents hoping to land a feature film gig. I do not see the appeal in making a lot of short films though and doing the whole festival game, to each their own though, have fun.

In *Night Swim* a former baseball player diagnosed with an illness moves into a new home with his family because it has a pool that he can use for therapy. After some swimming in the pool the man discovers that his degenerative disease is actually reversing course and he is convinced the water in the pool is healing him. It turns out that the pool is fed by an underground spring and while it has healing qualities it also requires payment in return, just ask all the damned souls that have been claimed by the pool and still lurk around doing spooky stuff.

Wyatt Russell is the father character Ray Waller. Wyatt is the son of Kurt Russell and Goldie Hawn. Kerry Condon plays his wife Eve Waller. Kerry Condon is Irish. The children who complete the family are Izzy Waller and Elliot Waller, portrayed by Amelie Hoeferle and Gavin Warren.

I think Russell was perfectly cast as the selfish ballplayer trying to figure out how to let go of his dreams and become a family man. He is not exactly a great guy but comes through in the end making for a strong, classic sort of character arc.

Kerry Condon's performance is also very strong as does a lot of the heavy lifting at the center of the story. If some other actress had been in the role and not been as compelling to watch the entire movie would have been forgettable junk perchance. There is a concept in storytelling called "saving the cat" where to get across to the audience that the person they are watching on screen is a good person that does a good deed early on, such as saving a cat. I thought it was cute that Eve Waller reaches into the dirty pool when they first see it and saves a cricket from drowning, immediately I thought that this was a "saving the cat" insertion.

Most child actors are not that great in movies in my grumbly old man opinion. However, the performances from Amelie Hoeferle and Gavin Warren were both solid. They really held up their ends, completing the Wallers as a family who is entertaining to watch as they realize their swimming pool is a dangerous thing.

Ray Waller was supposedly a major league baseball player with some talent before his illness made him quit. Therefore, when he is setting up his "man space" in the garage with his career mementos and such I thought the shrine a little weak. He just had a couple of shelves with some photos, a jersey, boxes, and trophies that looked Little League, not Big League. He pulls out a baseball card that was not well made either. As someone who follows baseball and even has some baseball cards from time to time I thought the details in this area were noticeably weak.

In the CGI ghost department, the results are a little silly as well. There is one fat guy ghost that arrives during "scary" parts and I did not find him scary at all. Actually, the movie is not scary at all and if one is looking for horror movie jump scares then maybe I oversold *Night Swim* to you with my early praise.

The story was enjoyable to me though and there were several cool moments. When Eve dives into the pool to try and save her son from the murky other dimension that is apparently there she ends up getting him but then is lost underwater. In the opening of the movie a little girl gets sucked into the pool and it was a nice touch to have her appear for the mother to show her the way out. She has one of the coins that the young boy was diving into the pool to get and she lets it go showing the mother which way is up and which way is down.

The dad is corrupted by the water and wants to sacrifice his son to it so that he can heal. I also liked the scene where he holds his wife in the air by her throat and his daughter approaches with a baseball bat. The mother told a story earlier in the film about some hand gestures she and her daughter would share to communicate and she uses those gestures in the moment to tell her daughter it is okay to whack daddy with the baseball bat.

One element I did find confusing was that the legend of the healing spring is that it grants one wish but then must take a sacrifice away before going dormant for some time. However, there is a previous lady that was once corrupted by the water in the past and she is shown still leaking the black stuff from her eyes and water seems to come to life in her house to cause trouble as well. I assumed that water from the pool was the magical element in play, not just water in general. A glass of water in the Waller home causes Izzy issues as well, making her slip and gets some glass into her hand.

The pool needed a sacrifice and chose the son character Elliot to serve as that. However, technically the pool had already taken a life from the family in the form of their cat Cider. Or at least it seemed like it took that cat. Yeah, greedy life devouring pool, do not trust it.

In the end Ray figures out how to save his son by sacrificing himself. He disappears into the water similar to how the little girl in the opening of the movie disappeared in order for her brother to get healed. Well, the girl did not make the choice her mother did. Anyway, my question with this is: how did the family explain the disappearance? There wasn't a drowned body? When Ray vanishes what was the story for the world?

The family does not move away from the house, instead electing to stay and have the pool filled in. I thought that this was the right choice for the story.

Night Swim is a decently crafted story and I enjoyed it. People who are afraid of drowning should get at least a little uncomfortable watching it but they don't really need to watch it though because I just rattled off a lot of the key scenes and spoiled the ending.

49. AMERICAN PSYCHO 2 - 2002

American Psycho 2: All American Girl is a movie that has me curious as to whether or not the screenplay is as stale of a turd as the movie itself is. Did the actors read it and think that it was great? Or did they not care and have other motivations? I have read articles claiming that the star Mila Kunis hates the movie because she did not know they were going to call it a sequel to *American Psycho* and it was altered after shooting but she does talk about Patrick Bateman in it, so, scenes were shot and dialog recorded with *American Psycho 2* in mind before the final edit.

You know who Morgan Freeman is right? Well, how about Morgan J. Freeman? The first one is an actor who starred in many beloved films. The second one directed American Psycho 2 which is a movie not more entertaining than poking at dog poop with a stick. I know: eww. Morgan J. Freeman also directed many other things including an episode of *Dawson's Creek* and the 1997 movie *Hurricane Streets*. I mention the teen drama *Hurricane Streets,* which he also wrote, out of all his credits because it is a movie I owned on VHS. It was a random purchase when I used to buy whatever used tapes were on sale at the rental store for a couple of bucks.

Alex Sanger and Karen Craig have the writing credits for this film. The screenplay was not originally a sequel project and started out with the title of *The Girl Who Wouldn't Die*. This appears to be the only writing credit for Alex Sanger and Karen Craig has only one other; bummer for them. As a writer I must repeat that I am curious about the original script and if it was as flawed as the story that was made into a moving picture. I have had scripts produced before and after watching the film I was left confused as to what the heck was going on. So, if that is the case, I know what that special disappointment feels like.

Mila Kunis stars as Rachael Newman though that is not her real name. She takes on another identity before the film ends as well. The character is someone who as a little girl was captured by the serial killer Patrick Bateman from *American Psycho*. However, she wiggled free from her bindings while he was busy killing her babysitter and she killed him. Then she grew up to be a psycho who kills a college student to take her place in a class being taught by the former FBI agent that was hunting Patrick Bateman as well as having been in a relationship with that dead babysitter. The teacher is Starkman as portrayed by William Shatner.

Kunis' character wants to become Starkman's teaching assistant because everyone knows his assistants also end up getting accepted into the FBI academy. In real life serial killers do often have an interest in law enforcement careers. I recall reading that Edmund Kemper couldn't get on the force, but he would hang out with cops frequently and after he committed his murders ended up calling them to turn himself in, disappointed that they weren't even looking for him. Rachael's stated motivation for joining the FBI is the only good thing in the movie. She wants to stop other psychos.

"I am killing for a better tomorrow."

And then she starts killing off the other students

that are her competition as well as anyone else that gets in her way. I am not sure how she even physically pulls off some of the kills, like there is a janitor that she sees and then the next time you see him his mop has been stabbed through his head and his body is in a dumpster. It escalates until she kills Starkman and then crashes a car with his corpse and Rachael Newman's corpse so that Newman takes the blame for everything and she can disappear. But—

—Kunis pops back up at the FBI as a lady named Elizabeth. She has taken over the identity of the previous teaching assistant that got accepted to the FBI. The entire journey makes zero sense as a story. Why didn't she just take the identity of THAT woman to begin with instead of going through all the gibberish and murdering? The ending seems like she is being crafty with a master plan having been executed, however, none of the events in the movie needed to happen for her to end up where she does.

Brian is a student competing with Rachael to become the teaching assistant. He is a terrible student but has the advantage of being rich and is going to buy the position. Why does he want to be an FBI agent? It doesn't sound like he would really want the gig or to do any work associated with it. Why would he go to great lengths spending his parents money to get the position when he could just live the life he wants spending money on other things? He gets strangled to death with a condom. Robin Dunne is the actor that portrays this character.

Lindy Booth is the character Cassandra. She is sleeping with Starkman to get the teaching position.

Rachael is able to hang her in her room and make it look like a suicide. How? It does not show her killing her.

Charles Officer portrays the character of Keith who is supposed to be the intelligent threat to steal the teaching position from Rachael. In the scene where he and Rachael are having a disagreement in class it is one of the dumbest shows of intellect one could have in that classroom setting. He states that he thinks Ted Bundy was an organized killer but Rachael argues that he was also disorganized due to his latter more frantic killings. If Keith knew his subject matter at all he would have known about Bundy's last victims and the entire argument would never have taken place. The class seems to be nothing more than students getting their serial killer trivia knowledge tested. Keith ends up getting stabbed to death in the library. It is weird that she kills him in public and then his murder just kind of doesn't get mentioned for a long while.

Rachael is really bad at covering her tracks throughout the movie and in the end even leaves her therapist alive knowing who she is and where to find her.

After Mila Kunis' character assumes a new identity and pins the killings on the real Rachel Newman there are a lot of news headlines with pictures covering the crimes. When they mention Rachael Newman though they do not show a picture of the deceased girl they show Mila Kunis.

One of the worst sins that *American Psycho 2* commits is that it is boring. The dialog and the acting are so bad at times that scenes are torture to sit through. Mila Kunis' voice became really annoying to me by the end of the film thanks to all of her voice over to go along with all of the other asinine blabber. Maybe you are a real horror pervert though and I just sold you on wanting to sit through it. Speed thee to Hell. Enjoy. Fans of the original should be horrified.

50. BLADE - 1998

Superhero movies were a joke when I was a kid. I watched Dolph Lundgren as *The Punisher* but did not find it better than *The Garbage Pail Kids Movie*. The 1990 *Captain America* movie didn't sell me on comic books as source material either. *Howard the Duck* was a goof we'd watch just to see duck boobies in the opening. (I wrote about *Howard the Duck* in my book titled *Movies Binge*.) The *Superman* movies were more success than not I think but they did not draw my interest away from the action flicks being pumped out void of superheroes. Then Tim Burton changed the numbers game with his two *Batman* films that I was a huge fan of, managed to get my parents to buy the VHS of the first film and line up in the McDonalds drive-thru to get our collector's soda cups. Batman was a DC property and even with the success his character was generating Marvel comics did not seem to ride his dark coattails with anything. Stallone did a *Judge Dredd* movie in 1995 and while we rented it now and then it was no *Demolition Man*. I can recall the 1997 *Spawn* movie was not as good as its soundtrack. *Blade* released in 1998 and Wesley Snipes was exactly the right actor for the role. I was a Snipes fan and aside from *Demolition Man* I remember *Passenger 57* being a favorite rental. Also, my name is Wesley and when you are young it is fun to see famous people who share your name. *Blade* is where my memory sees a Marvel property getting put on the cinematic map. Marvel would eventually go on to rule theaters with *Spider-man*, *Avengers*, *Iron Man*, and such but the *Blade* franchise was what drew a non-comic book fan like me into one of their universes. It was the horror elements that made *Blade* so cool. Vampires were big in the 90s. One could argue that the horror genre is to be thanked for Marvel becoming the superhero film behemoth that it did. I know, that is a stretch, but how about this: horror movie villains are actually just superheroes too. Think about Jason and Freddy, indestructible with special abilities, yeah, that's no different than Superman! Comic book film history, DC film history, Marvel film history, the intersections where horror and comic book movies meet, I think that there is a whole book concept circling around in this opening paragraph.

As a character Blade first appeared in the 70s as a supporting character in *The Tomb of Dracula*. The character would be altered quite a bit for the film version and I bet that the version crafted by Hollywood is more familiar to folks than the original. David S. Goyer helped transform Blade when he wrote the screenplay for the feature. He has written the scripts for a lot of popular movies and has directed some as well. In 2004 *Blade: Trinity* became the second feature film that Goyer directed.

Stephen Norrington directed *Blade*. This film was his second full feature to direct after the 1994 horror film *Death Machine* starring Chucky himself, Mr. Brad Dourif. Norrington does not actually have a lot of directorial credits at the time of my writing this. It seems like the 2003 film *The League of Extraordinary Gentlemen* might have derailed his career in that regard. Hollywood loves you one day, hates you the next as the movie tickets and dollar bills get stacked.

Blade is a vampire hunter who has "all of their powers and none of their weaknesses." His mother was bitten by a vampire and gave birth to him, passing along the elements to make him half human and half vampire. He suppressed his thirst for human blood using a special serum that is growing weaker over time. The villain for the film is Deacon Frost, an ambitious vampire seeking to break with the pureblood traditions of his people in order to rule over all humans. He seeks to fulfill a prophecy that will imbue him with the powers of La Magra the blood God.

Wesley Snipes portrays Blade as the ultimate badass. Both he and his helper Whistler, portrayed by Kris Kristofferson, have been at their work for long enough that they are somewhat cold and blunt when it comes to dealing with people outside their two man operation. However, as a part of his character arc Blade is put back in touch with the emotions of his human side and has to deal with such a "weakness." Whistler also takes a moment to let it be known that he is not as heartless as he conducts himself and shares the same walls that Blade puts up in order to shield himself from being overwhelmed by a tragedy from his past. Both Snipes and Kristofferson are perfect in their roles.

When I talk about Blade being all about business I do not mean that he is void of personality, however. In the very first action scene that he is introduced in he shows flashes of the playful ego within. He makes his work fun with wise-ass smiles and posing flair. I think that this movie crafted Blade as an easy character to build a franchise around. I am a fan.

"You used me as bait?"

"Get over it."

N'Bushe Wright portrays Karen, the woman who enters Blade's life and inspires him to be more in touch with his human side. He brings her home as a "stray" after he sees her bitten and thinks about the mother he lost. Karen reminds him of himself and I would reckon that he has some sexual attraction to her as well, even though there is not a romantic subplot. In a late scene of the movie Blade is in need of power rejuvenation—as a vampire he needs his serum or his blood, and Klaren gives herself to him to feed upon. Even though there is not a direct romantic subplot I think that Blade sucking the blood out of Karen was shot as a love making scene with her gasps and moans maybe driving that point across a little too obvious. Also, I must note, that after he feeds on her she goes about participating in some action sequences when I would have thought her to have been a bit more woozy. And it might be a little too convenient for the story that Karen happens to be a hematologist when Blade is dealing with blood issues ala vampirism is akin to having a blood disease. It then seems odd that he and Whistler never thought to seek out someone like her in the past considering how quick she is able to make progress toward helping their work and crafting an actual cure too.

N'Bushe Wright is not an actress who has been in a lot of movies that I have seen. However, the movie *Dead Presidents* from 1995 is an action drama that I used to rent frequently and she is the memorable character Delilah in that.

Stephen Dorff is the villain Deacon Frost and it is

another example of perfect casting. Frost is an ambitious young jerk that while being identifiable in his wish to make his own way in the world never overshadows the cool wreaking machine that is Blade. I have read that Jet Li was almost cast as Frost; what a different movie that would have been.

    Donal Logue is the right-hand man of Frost named Quinn. He is all about having a good time and keeps getting his arms lopped off by Blade. The arm chopping gag reminds me of Paul "Pee-Wee Herman" Reubens getting his arm cut off in the 1992 movie *Buffy the Vampire Slayer* as the character Amilyn.

    The other vampire that hangs out with Frost that really steals one's attention when she is in a scene is Mercury portrayed by Arly Jover. When I call her scene stealing I do not mean in the acting department, her character does not have a lot to do but visually she really stamps the time period that this film was made in and when my mind thinks of *Blade* I am quick to recall her and how she exudes 90s "cool girl" vibes moving through scenes. Born in Melilla, Spain, Arly Jover came to America to study ballet in New York City. I am not sure how the transition to acting occurred but having *Blade* as one's feature debut is impressive. She can also be seen in the 2002 bloodsucker movie *Vampires: Los Muertos*.

    The horror elements make this film what it is. Yes, the action is entertaining but the blood and horror visuals allowed by the R rating are what set *Blade* apart from the pack. The blood usage in the opening is epic with enough of the red stuff to drown out any genre snobs that might not want to classify *Blade* as a horror movie. While technically a scene showing Blade being born is the opening of the movie, the dance club scene is the opening of the movie that is going to stick with you.

Traci Lords is a female vampire named in the credits as Racquel. The only work that she does in this movie is to lure a human date to a vampire rave club that is located inside of a meat packing plant. It sounds like anyone could have filled the shoes for the role but the fact is that Lords exudes some on camera presence that is stellar. When she is paired with Arly Jover on the dance floor it is easy to see how vampires can be regarded as sexy even with their nasty taste for blood.

If you are not familiar with Traci Lords she has quite the interesting story regarding her path to mainstream Hollywood. Born in Ohio as Nora Louise Kuzma, she became an actress in pornographic films at a very young age, an illegal to be appearing in porn age, that caused quite the industry stir when the information came to light. I am not sure how many porn films Lords participated in during the 80s but I have read that only one is technically legal in the United States. So, if you have been watching Traci Lords porn not titled *Traci, I Love You* understand that it was the only one filmed after her eighteenth birthday.

Tim Guinee portrays the guy, Curtis Webb, who is lured into the club in the beginning of *Blade*. Akin to how I said that Arly Jover screams "90s woman" this Webb character screams "90s tryhard." He seems like a guy trying too hard to be cool but the way he is treated by the people in the club, his date ditches him, made me quick to feel sorry for him. When the blood starts spraying out of the sprinkler system and the dancing vampires start to snarl at him the man seems doomed but this is when

Blade arrives to save the day. It is such a fun opening.

The vampire Quinn gets lit on fire in the dance club scene and his charred corpse is taken to the hospital where Karen works. This is how Karne ends up getting bitten and the sight of the burnt Quinn coming to life is the second strong horror moment that I enjoy a lot. The blackened vampire running around in the hospital is scary stuff for the eyes and not the type of Marvel family content the glossy *Avengers* movies and such brought to market.

Another moment with blood play that I really like is when Frost bites into one of his human helpers. The blood gushes and Mercury moves over to get a taste as well. Frost and Mercury lick each other's mouths with greed and the gore drips.

It is also hard to forget the obese vampire Pearl, a real Jabba the Hutt, that lounges around investigating vampire history for Frost. Blade and Karen go to Pearl for information and the way that they extract it is by torturing the creature with a UV flashlight. Pearl's screams and the way its flesh burns are fun nightmare material.

He might be called the "daywalker" but Blade zooms around in this movie in a 1968 Dodge Charger R/T. I am by no means a car buff but I absolutely think that old muscle cars are the coolest in design. I can't tell you what a car is by its official name but I can see the vehicle and state: "That's the car from Blade." As for the term "daywalker," I use it frequently because I tend to keep "vampire hours" and when I am able to flip to being awake during "normal" hours I tend to proclaim my status as being a daywalker. So, *Blade* has given me something that is a part of my lifeline vocabulary I suppose. Now if I can just get someone to give me the car as well.

There are a lot of good lines in *Blade* but I have to say that my favorite one is what Blade delivers in the final showdown against Frost: "Some motherfuckers are always trying to ice-skate uphill."

When the film first came out the CGI effects in some spots did not impress me. On this 2024 viewing of the 4K disc I assumed that all the visual effects would look too silly. When the vampires turn into ash I think that this effect holds up well enough. There are some odd-looking flames here and there and when the vampires have flying skeletons rip out of them in the final sequences the limits are being pushed regarding whether or not someone might not be able to take the movie seriously due to dated graphics. However, the worst looking effects are when Frost gets his blood god powers. This specific moment NEVER looked good in the film and nothing has changed. At one point Blade cuts Frost in half and his body is repaired by blood and the dated computer technology is very obvious. Also, when Frost is defeated he balloons up into a blood red mess that makes for another weak visual. It stinks that the worst effects happen in these most important moments.

Frost wishes to become a blood god in the film, which was a motive that I understood, ultimate power is a classic villain desire. At one point though he mentions that everyone in the world will be turned into vampires after the ceremony. I got confused by this statement because he calls humans cattle and wants to rule them. If they turn all humans into vampires then what will they eat? I have read that there was an explanation to clarify this with some humans being stored for a food source but as it was presented in the film it is a plot hole of sorts. Personally, I think they should have left those lines out if they could have and just have had the goal being ultimate power. Or as Quinn says: "I'm gonna be naughty. I'm gonna be a naughty vampire god."

In the end I think I have perhaps seen *Blade* too many times but it is still a strong action horror hybrid. It is like those one potato chip ads with a person not being able to stop eating after just one—this film makes me want to watch the rest of the original trilogy now.

"The world you live in is just a sugar-coated topping! There is another world beneath it: the real world. And if you wanna survive it, you better learn to pull the trigger!"

"There are worse things out tonight than vampires."

"Like what?"

"Like me."

www.ingramcontent.com/pod-product-compliance
Lightning Source LLC
Chambersburg PA
CBHW052246220526
45471CB00001B/207